The British North America Act 1867

THE GREAT CANADIAN TAX HOAX

The Unconstitutionality of
Unlimited Federal Provincial
Transfer Payments

BURTON H. KELLOCK Q.C.

Copyright © 2020 Burton H. Kellock Q.C

All rights reserved. No part of this publication may be reproduced or transmitted in any form or by any means, electronic or mechanical, including photocopying, recording, or any information storage and retrieval system, without permission in writing from the author.

Published in 2020 by
Kinetics Design, KDbooks.ca
ISBN 978-1-988360-40-9 (paperback)
ISBN 978-1-988360-41-6 (ebook)

Cover and interior design, typesetting and printing by Daniel Crack,
Kinetics Design, KDbooks.ca
linkedin.com/in/kdbooks/

Contact the author at
Burt Kellock <burtkellock@gmail.com>

CONTENTS

Introduction   7
   Author's Note   11

CHAPTER 1
How "Constitutionality" is Determined   13

CHAPTER 2
The History of the BNA Act, Its Important Provisions and Their Judicial Interpretation   18

CHAPTER 3
The History of Federal/Provincial Transfer Payments   44

CHAPTER 4
The Proponent's Propositions   65
   Part I
   The Proponents' Arguments   65

   Part 2
   The C.L.O.C.'s Arguments   81

CHAPTER 5
Conclusions   93

AN ACT

OF THE IMPERIAL PARLIAMENT

FOR THE

UNION

OF

CANADA, NOVA SCOTIA AND NEW BRUNSWICK,

AND THE

GOVERNMENT THEREOF;
AND FOR PURPOSES CONNECTED THEREWITH.

(30 *VICTORIÆ*, *CAP*. 3.)

OTTAWA:
PRINTED BY HUNTER, ROSE & CO.
1867.

The Constitution Act 1867

Introduction

THE purpose of this book is to debunk the entirely baseless proposition that unlimited Federal/Provincial fiscal transfers ("F.P.F.T.") are authorized by the Canadian Constitution and therefore lawful. I will call those who assert the truth of this proposition, "the Proponents."

The Constitution of Canada today, consists largely of two British statutes, *The British North America Act 1867* ("The *BNA Act*"), now named *The Constitution Act 1867* and the *Constitution Act 1982*. Both are British statutes and have never been amended.

At the time the *BNA Act* was enacted by the Parliament of the U.K., Canada was a British Colony ruled from Westminster. As such, the *BNA Act* could only be amended by the British Parliament. With the enactment of the *Constitution Act 1982* (another British statute), both the *BNA Act* (which was renamed the *Constitution Act 1867*) and the *Constitution Act 1982* became amendable in Canada, but as noted neither has been changed by amendment or otherwise.

The purpose of the *BNA Act* was to establish "Canada" as a "Federal State", which is to say, "a system in which states unite under a central authority but are independent in internal affairs."[1] The *BNA Act* created a new state in British North America to be called "Canada." As Canada was to be a "federal" state with a central or Federal government as well

---

1 Oxford Dictionary.

as Provincial governments, it was necessary for the *BNA Act* to delineate the governmental powers to be exercisable by the Federal Parliament on the one hand, and the Provincial Parliaments or Legislative Assemblies on the other. It is therefore not surprising that provisions of the *BNA Act* are largely devoted to that delineation.

It is now usual to describe the Federal and Provincial governments as two "levels" of government, but this is the result of the entirely erroneous assumption that the Federal government is the pre-eminent authority and the Provincial governments are in some way subservient. Nothing could be further from the truth.

Both the government in Ottawa and the governments located in the provincial capitals each have their own *independent* powers to levy taxes, and neither is authorized to raise money by taxation for the support of the other with one, and only one specific and severely limited exception, which is to found in section 118 which I will discuss fully in due course. That is why the division of powers provisions of the *BNA Act* constitute the key to understanding why F.P.F.T. are unauthorized. It is obvious that if F.P.F.T. were constitutional, the Provincial governments would not be independent, and Canada could not therefore be regarded as a "federal state" as the dictionary defines it.

As we shall see, the *BNA Act* was enacted in 1867 to implement the agreement reached by the representatives of the then Canadian Provinces at a meeting held at Quebec City in 1864. They are now known, for obvious reasons, as the "Fathers" of Canadian Confederation. As of 1867, in the event that any doubt as to the meaning of any of the provisions of the *BNA Act* should arise, the rule of law to be applied to resolve that doubt was clear, and of very long standing. It was stated by Sir Edward Coke (pronounced "Cook") in his *Institutes of the Laws of England* published between 1628 and 1644. Coke said that the task of the judiciary in interpreting an Act was to seek to interpret it, according to the intent of them that made it,"[2] and them that made the *BNA Act* are the Fathers of Confederation. That was the rule in Coke's time, and it remains the rule today.

Consequently, all that is necessary to know and understand why it is

---

[2] Coke 4 Inst. 330 cited with approval by Viscount Dilhorne in the judgment of the House of Lords in *Stock v. Frank Jones (Tipton) Ltd.* (1978) 1 W.L.R. 231 at 234.

that the Parliament of Canada has no authority whatsoever to authorize F.P.F.T. is to be found in the records of the Quebec Conference, first published by Sir Joseph Pope in 1895, and now conveniently set forth in Professor Browne's book entitled "Documents on the Confederation of British North America."[3] That is where you will find what them that made the *BNA Act* intended concerning F.P.F.T..

For reasons which I cannot even begin to explain, the Proponents are entirely ignorant of the proceedings of the Quebec Conference and the decisions made there, as to what the Canadian Constitution would and would not provide for, in respect to F.P.F.T., which renders their opinions absolutely worthless.

The leading proponent today is Dr. Peter Hogg, a former Dean of the Osgoode Hall Law School at York University and the author of a textbook entitled (not surprisingly) "Constitutional Law of Canada." I will refer hereinafter to that work as "C.L.O.C." In C.L.O.C., the author states that the power of the Federal government to authorize F.P.F.T. "is nowhere explicit" in the *BNA Act*, but that is not correct. C.L.O.C. goes on to assert that because the power to authorize F.P.F.T. is not explicit "it must be implied," which is to say "read into" the *BNA Act*.

It *must* be read in (says Professor Hogg) because the *BNA Act* empowers Parliament to levy taxes, to legislate in relation to "public property" and to "appropriate (i.e. authorize the spending of, federal funds.") That assertion is sheer nonsense.

As noted, C.L.O.C's assertion that the transfer of Federal tax money to the Provinces is "nowhere explicit in the *BNA Act*," is false. It is clearly false as anyone who has read sections 102, 118 and 126 of the *BNA Act* can see. Section 102 is to be found in the *BNA Act* under the heading "Revenues; Debts; Assets; Taxation," which provides as follows:

> "*VIII. REVENUES; DEBTS; ASSETS; TAXATION*
>
> 102. *All Duties and Revenues over which the respective Legislatures of Canada, Nova Scotia, and New Brunswick before and at the Union had and have Power of Appropriation, except such Portions thereof as are by this Act reserved to the respective Legislatures of the provinces, or are raised by them in accordance with the special*

---

3 Carleton Library series 215, McGill-Queens University Press (2009).

> *Powers conferred on them by this Act, shall form One Consolidated Revenue Fund, to be appropriated for the Public Service of Canada in the Manner and subject to the Charges in this Act provided."*

An appropriation is quite simply a governmental authorization to spend money.

As this provision was drafted before the *BNA Act* came into force, the powers of appropriation it provides for are those which at the time section 102 was drafted, belonged to the then Provinces that existed before Confederation, which, when united, by Confederation, would produce the new state of "Canada." Prior to Confederation, the word "Canada" had been the name given to the then Province of Canada, which was created in 1840 by the union of the former Provinces of Upper and Lower Canada. Those former Provinces became, after Confederation, the Provinces of Ontario and Quebec.

Once the *BNA Act* came into force, "Canada" became a new federal state comprised of what had formerly been the Provinces of Canada, Nova Scotia and New Brunswick. This is made clear by the provisions of section 126 of the *BNA Act*.

> "**126.** *Such Portions of the Duties and Revenues over which the respective Legislatures of Canada, Nova Scotia and New Brunswick had before the Union Power of Appropriation as are by this Act reserved to the respective Governments or Legislatures of the provinces, and all Duties and Revenues raised by them in accordance with the special Powers conferred upon them by this Act, shall in each Province form One Consolidated Revenue Fund to be appropriated for the Public Service of the Province."*

There cannot be any doubt whatsoever that the "Public Service of Canada" was *not* to be the public service of any Province and that after confederation, all money raised by Federal taxation could be spent only for the Public Service of Canada (the new country) and all money raised by Provincial taxes could only be spent for the public service of the province which had raised the money. Accordingly, no money whatsoever that was raised for the Public Service of Canada could be spent for the Public Service of a Province except as provided for in Section 118, which will be discussed hereinafter.

To say, as C.L.O.C. does, that the spending power of the Federal government "is nowhere explicit" in the *BNA Act* is a fundamental and egregious error, which is inexplicable. I cannot even imagine how the author of C.L.O.C. could make such an error or that sections 102 and 126 of the *BNA Act* are *deliberately* and *entirely* omitted from the version of the *BNA Act* which is attached to C.L.O.C. as an appendix to it and advertised as the "*Constitution Act* 1867." That Appendix is not the *Constitution Act 1867*. It is, instead the *Constitution Act 1867 minus* sections 102 and 126.

But sections 102 and 126 of the *BNA Act* do exist. They have existed since July 1, 1867 when the *BNA Act* came into force and *have never been repealed or amended*.

The omission from C.L.O.C. of these sections is not explained anywhere in the text of C.L.O.C. The absence of those sections and any explanation for their omission can only be described as egregious.

Author's Note

This book is about the Federal government's "spending power."

From its birth in 1867 until now, the power to make laws in Canada (the legislative power) is conferred by and limited by the British statute, (originally entitled) "*The British North American Act 1867*," now the *Constitution Act 1867* — the *BNA Act*.

Since the day that the English landowners confronted King John at Runnymede in 1215, the British government could not impose any tax on any citizen without the authorization of the British Parliament. The *BNA Act* made that the rule in Canada for both the Federal and Provincial governments. Likewise, no British or Canadian government can take a penny out of its treasury (where the tax money must be deposited) without Parliament's consent.

Our first Prime Minister, Sir John A. Macdonald, when a member of the group of politicians (now known as the Fathers of Confederation) which drafted the *BNA Act* put a motion to the group at a meeting held at Quebec City in 1866 suggesting that the *BNA Act* should authorize the Federal Parliament to make grants (out of the money it raised from federal taxpayers) to the governments of the Provinces. That motion was defeated. Consequently, the constitution of Canada prohibits any and all F.P.F.T. Federal/Provincial transfer payments, save for one explicitly stated exception, and has always done so. Those who have in the past and continue to argue that F.P.F.T. are lawful (the "Proponents") are completely unaware of this crucial aspect of the history of the *BNA Act*. Accordingly, none of them have even suggested how F.P.F.T., which are not authorized by the Canadian Constitution and therefore prohibited, can be regarded as anything but a violation of it.

As a result of the Proponents abysmal ignorance, billions upon billions, indeed trillions of dollars have been unlawfully extracted from the pockets of Canadian taxpayers for 162 years. What follows is the tragic story of how Canada was founded (and continues to be based) on ignorance. That is not something any Canadian can be proud of.

The proverb, "When ignorance is bliss, it is folly to be wise" (which comes from the English poet Thomas Gray in a passage from "On a Distant Prospect of Eton College"), is absolutely untrue. Thus, Canada has been a state sustained by ignorance.

CHAPTER 1

How "Constitutionality" is Determined

Constitutional Law of Canada (C.L.O.C.), the leading textbook on its subject, defines its title as follows:

> *"Constitutional law is the law prescribing the exercise of powers by the organs of a State. It explains which organs can exercise legislative power (making new laws), executive power (implementing the laws) and judicial power (adjudicating disputes), and what the limitations on those powers are. In a federal state, the allocation of governmental powers, (legislative, executive and judicial), among central and regional (state or provincial) authorities is a basic concern. The rules of federalism are especially significant in Canada because they protect the cultural, linguistic and regional diversity of the nation. Civil liberties are also part of constitutional law, because civil liberties may be created by the rules that limit the exercise of governmental power over individuals. A constitution has been described as "a mirror reflecting the national soul" it must recognize and protect the values of a nation."*[4]

From Canada's birth in 1867 to date, the *BNA Act* has been the sole constitutional source of the "rules of federalism." Those rules allocate all governmental powers in Canada (Legislative, executive and judicial) among the federal and Provincial governments.[5]

---

4 C.L.O.C. Section 1.1.
5 C.L.O.C. Section 1.2.

In addition to "the rules of federalism," Canada was also to have "a Constitution similar in principle to that of the United Kingdom," as stated in the preamble to the *BNA Act*, and so, as C.L.O.C. states:

> "The British North Americans wanted the old rules to continue in both form and substance exactly as before."

Accordingly, the old rules (which implemented the principles of the British Constitution) have been a part of Canada's "Constitutional Law" from the beginning. For example, the Canadian Constitution includes the principle of "legality," known as the "Rule of Law."[6] Part I of the *Constitution Act 1982* explicitly states that "Canada is founded upon principles that recognize the Supremacy of God and the rule of law."

C.L.O.C. goes on to state that:

> "The Constitution must be "Supreme" meaning that it must be binding on and unalterable by each of the central and regional authorities. If either could unilaterally change the distribution of powers, then the authorities would not be coordinate: Supreme power would lie with the authority having the power to change the Constitution. The same idea is sometimes expressed by saying that a federal constitution must be "rigid" (or "entrenched"). The term "rigid" does not imply that it cannot be amended ... but it does imply that the power-distributing parts of the Constitution cannot be amended by ordinary legislative action: a special and more difficult process is required for amendment."

For most amendments to the Constitution, Part V (of the *Constitution Act 1982*) requires the assents of the two houses of the federal Parliament and two-thirds of the provincial legislative assemblies representing 50 percent of the population of all of the Provinces. This "entrenchment" of the Constitution makes it "rigid."[7]

As one of the primary purposes of a Constitution is to explain "which organs of a state" can exercise legislative power,[8] it is obvious that any and all amendments to the *BNA Act* (or *The Constitution Act, 1982*) must be made by a legislature with the jurisdiction so to do. From 1867

---

6 C.L.O.C. Section 1.1.
7 C.L.O.C. Section 5.4.
8 C.L.O.C. Section 1.1

until 1982, that legislature was the British parliament at Westminster. It is equally obvious that unless the language of the Constitution is changed by formal amendment, the meaning of that language cannot change either. In a democracy, the laws are made or changed by a legislature consisting of those who have been elected to exercise the legislative function of government. No one else has any authority to change the language or meaning of the Constitution. The function of the judiciary is to interpret, which is to say to declare, the meaning of the language used by the legislators, not to change it.

There has never been any change to the provisions of the *BNA Act* relating to Parliament's authority to make F.P.F.T. since 1907.

The highest Court of Appeal for Canadian cases from 1867 until 1949, the Judicial Committee of the British Privy Council, decided on more than one occasion that the parliament of Canada's spending power was confined to funding policies and programs otherwise within federal jurisdiction so that no federal tax money could be devoted to funding any policies or programs within the legislative jurisdiction of the Provinces.

As C.L.O.C. acknowledges, this was because:

> "The framers (the Fathers of Confederation) were accustomed to look to the Judicial Committee of the Privy Council in England as the final appellate authority for British North America ... and they were content to leave the appellate authority in those safe British hands."[9]

It was those "safe British hands" which from 1867 until 1949 determined whether or not a federal or provincial statute was *intra vires* (within the power) or *ultra vires* (beyond the power) of the enacting legislature (whether federal or provincial). If *intra vires* the legislation was constitutionally valid, if *ultra vires* it was void.

This has always been the case and is re-stated in section 52(1) of the *Constitution Act 1982*:

> "52(1) The Constitution of Canada is the Supreme law of Canada, and any law that is inconsistent with the provisions of the

---

9 C.L.O.C. Section 1.2.

> *Constitution is, to the extent of the inconsistency, of no force or effect."*

In the section of C.L.O.C. entitled "Case Law" the author has this to say:

> *"The courts have the task of interpreting the Constitution Acts and the other constitutional statutes. Their decisions constitute precedents for later cases so that a body of judge-made or decisional law, usually called case law, develops in areas where there has been litigation. While the courts' role is simply one of interpretation, the cumulative effect of a series of precedents will constitute and important elaboration or even modification of the original text. In particular, the provisions of the Constitution Act, 1867 that distribute legislative power between the central Parliament and the provincial Legislatures are now overlaid by such an accumulation of cases that it would be unthinkable to attempt to ascertain the relevant rules by recourse to the Act alone."* [10]

That statement is not entirely accurate. The word "modify" means making "minor changes to," but no court in the common law world (which includes Canada) has any jurisdiction whatsoever to change the language that the people's elected representatives have chosen to implement the policies that only they are entitled to make law. If the language of that law is to be "modified," it must be modified by a legislature. It cannot be modified by one Judge or a thousand Judges. While Judges have the jurisdiction to declare what the language of the law means, no Judge has jurisdiction to "declare" what the language of a legislative instrument should mean, or what a Judge would like it to mean.

On the precedent-setting nature of decisions by higher courts, C.L.O.C. states that:

> *"Canadian courts accept the doctrine of precedent (or stare decisis) under which the decisions of a court are binding on courts lower in the judicial hierarchy."*

However, it is one thing to say that prior judicial decisions are "binding" and quite another to say that the principle of *stare decisis* is

---

10 C.L.O.C. Section 1.8.

always scrupulously observed. If the Supreme Court of Canada, which is now the court of last resort for Canadian cases, should depart from prior judicial decisions made by the Privy Council or the Supreme Court itself, there is no higher court to appeal to.

To quote Justice Robert Jackson (a former member of the Supreme Court of the U.S.):

> "We are not final because we are infallible. We are infallible because we final."

Justice Jackson's comment is completely accurate. As there is no longer a right to appeal form the decisions of the Supreme Court of Canada to the Privy Council or any other tribunal, the Supreme Court's decisions are binding upon all of us unless and until they are changed by a subsequent decision of that court or an amendment to the Constitution. To re-phrase Jackson's remark, the Supreme Court's decisions are binding, not because they are right or even presumed to be right, but simply because there may be no way to correct them.

The key decisions concerning parliament's authority to make F.P.F.T were delivered many years ago by the Privy Council when it, not the Supreme Court of Canada, was final and therefore infallible.

Consequently, the provisions of our Constitutional law concerning the existence or non-existence of Parliament's authority to authorize federal/provincial transfers as part of its "spending power" is the supposedly "rigid" provisions of the *BNA Act* as interpreted by the binding decisions of the Privy Council and (since 1949) the Supreme Court of Canada. The rigidity of the division of powers provisions of the Canadian Constitution may be perceived to be inconvenient by many politicians and others who would like the Constitution to provide for federal/provincial transfers. But as it doesn't so provide, the rule of law requires everyone including the Federal government to abide by the Constitution as written, unless and until it is changed in the only lawful way it can be changed, by amendment.

CHAPTER 2

The History of the BNA Act, Its Important Provisions and Their Judicial Interpretation

The appropriation (spending) of federal money, whether intended to be transferred to a Provincial government or used for any other purpose, may only be affected by legislation, i.e. the enactment by the Parliament of Canada of a constitutionally valid *Appropriation Act*.

To be valid, a federal *Appropriation Act* must be a law made "in relation to" a subject matter that the *BNA Act* places within the law-making authority of the Parliament of Canada. Needless to say, the Federal government will not have any money to appropriate for any purpose unless it has been raised by a constitutionally valid federal tax.[11]

In its judgment in the 2014 *Senate Reform* case,[12] the Supreme Court of Canada held that the *BNA Act* was to be interpreted according to these rules:

> "1. The Constitution must be interpreted with a view to discerning the structure of government it seeks to implement. The assumptions that underlie the text and the manner in which the constitutional provisions are intended to

---

11 Which like federal spending must be authorized by laws made in relation to a subject within Parliament's legislative authority.
12 Reference *Re: Senate Reform*, [2014] S.C.C. 22.

interact with one another must inform our interpretation, understanding, and application of the text," and

"2. The Courts look to whether legislation, in its purpose and effects, falls within one of the classes of subjects over which the Constitution gives power to the enacting body."

If an *Appropriation Act*, which is required to raise and spend money to be transferred to a province, does not fall within one of the classes of subjects over which the Constitution (i.e. the *BNA Act*) gives the power to legislate to the Parliament of Canada, it follows that an *Appropriation Act* which is inconsistent with the provisions of the Constitution is of no force or effect by reason of section 52(1) of the *Constitution Act 1982*. Such legislation is described in law as *ultra vires*, i.e. beyond Parliament's power to enact.

In the case of federal transfer payments, one of the "assumptions" that "must inform the interpretation" of the text of the *BNA Act* is that the Fathers deliberately decided that Parliament would not have the authority to make laws respecting *"subsidies or grants in aid of the (Provinces)"* other than the transfers required to be made by section 118.

The importance of the Fathers' assumptions was further explained in 1980 by the Supreme Court of Canada in its judgment in *Reference Re: The Legislative Authority of the Parliament of Canada in relation to the Upper House*.[13]

The question to be decided in the *Upper House* case was whether or not Parliament possessed the constitutional authority to enact legislation altering or providing a replacement for the Senate.

To understand the assumptions the Fathers had made with respect to the role of the Senate, the Court quoted from the speeches made in the Parliament of the Province of Canada, which followed the Quebec Conference, by Sir John A. Macdonald (Conservative) and George Brown (Liberal) as to why Resolution 6 provided that the "general Legislature or Parliament for the federated Provinces" was to be "composed of a Legislative Council (the Upper House or Senate) and a House of Commons."

Both Macdonald and Brown made it clear that the constitutional

---

13 [1980] 1 S.C.R. 54.

purpose of the Senate was to provide representation for the three geographical regions in which Canada was then separated, being "1. Upper Canada (now Ontario). 2. Lower Canada (now Quebec), and 3. Nova Scotia, New Brunswick and Prince Edward Island." Each was to have "equal representation" in the Parliament of Canada.

The court then drew these conclusions:[14]

> *"A primary purpose of the creation of the Senate, as a part of the federal legislative process, was ... to afford protection to the various sectional interests in Canada in relation to the enactment of federal legislation.*
>
> *The creation of a federal system in Canada involved the necessity of effecting a division of legislative powers. This division is made by the provisions of ss. 91 and 92 of the Act. The latter section empowered each provincial legislature generally to make laws, effective within the province, in respect of matters of a local or private nature. Fifteen specific classes of subject were enumerated.*
>
> *Section 91 provided generally for the making of laws for the peace, order and good Government of Canada. Twenty-nine classes of subject matters were enumerated. Legislation dealing with those matters might affect local or private matters within a province.*[15]
>
> *The power to enact federal legislation was given to the Queen by and with the advice and consent of the Senate and the House of Commons. Thus, the body which had been created as a means of protecting sectional and provincial interests was made a participant in this legislative process.*
>
> *Bearing in mind the historical background in which the creation of the Senate as a part of the federal legislative process was conceived, the words of Lord Sankey L.C. in Re The Regulation and Control of Aeronautics in Canada,*[16] *although they were written in relation to the Act as originally enacted, are apt:*

---

14 pp. 66-68.

15 In other words, federal legislation if enacted lawfully pursuant to Sections 91 were to be considered constitutionally valid, even if the legislation "might affect" subject matters assigned by Section 92 to provincial jurisdiction.

16 26 [1932] A.C. 54.

> *Inasmuch as the Act embodies a compromise under which the original provinces agreed to federate, it is important to keep in mind that the preservation of the rights of minorities was a condition on which such minorities entered into the federation, and the foundation upon which the whole structure was subsequently erected. The process of interpretation as the years go on ought not be allowed to dim or to whittle down the provisions of the original contract upon which the federation was founded, nor is it legitimate that any judicial construction of the provisions of ss. 91 and 92 should impose a new and different contract upon the federating bodies."*

In the light of this statement it is not surprising that the Supreme Court held in the *Upper House* case that the provisions of the Constitution relating to the Senate could not be unilaterally altered by the federal Parliament.

In 1998 the Supreme Court again referred to the Quebec Conference in the Reference regarding the possibility of the separation of Quebec,[17] and the following statement is part of its judgment, in that case:

> *"The Quebec Conference began on October 10, 1864. Thirty-three delegates (two from Newfoundland, seven from New Brunswick, five from Nova Scotia, seven from Prince Edward Island, and twelve from the Province of Canada) met over a two- and a half-week period. Precise consideration of each aspect of the federal structure preoccupied the political agenda. The delegates approved 72 resolutions, addressing almost all of what subsequently made its way into the final text of the Constitution Act 1867. These included guarantees to protect French language and culture, both directly (by making French an official language in Quebec and Canada as a whole) and indirectly (by allocating jurisdiction over education and 'Property and Civil Rights in the Province' to the provinces). The protection of minorities was thus reaffirmed.*
>
> *Legally, there remained only the requirement to have the Quebec Resolutions put into proper form and passed by the Imperial Parliament in London. However, politically, it was thought that more was required. Indeed, Resolution 70 provided that "The Sanction of the Imperial and Local Parliaments shall be sought*

---

17 Reference *Re: Secession of Quebec*, [1998] 2 S.C.R. 217 at 242.

for the Union of the provinces, on the principles adopted by the Conference." (Cited in J. Pope, ed, Confederation: Being a Series of Hitherto Unpublished Documents Bearing on the British North America Act (1985), at p. 52 (emphasis added)).

Confirmation of the Quebec Resolutions was achieved more smoothly in central Canada than in the Maritimes. In February and March 1865, the Quebec Resolutions were the subject of almost six weeks of sustained debate in both houses of the Canadian legislature. The Canadian Legislative Assembly approved the Quebec Resolutions in March 1865 with the support of a majority of members from both Canada East and Canada West. The governments of both Prince Edward Island and Newfoundland chose, in accordance with popular sentiment in both colonies, not to accede to the Quebec Resolutions."

Notwithstanding the Supreme Court's judgment in the *Upper House* case, Parliament tried again in 2013 to change the provisions of the *BNA Act* relating to the Senate. It sought the Supreme court's opinion as to whether it might change the composition of the Senate or abolish it entirely. The court responded by reiterating the point it had made in the Quebec Secession Reference, that "The Constitution implements a structure of government and must be understood by reference to the constitutional text, the historical context and previous judicial interpretation, of constitutional meaning."[18] In other words (as Coke said) "according to the intent of them that made it."

It is therefore abundantly clear that the answer to what might be supposed to be "legal" questions, such as the nature of the Senate and its constitutional role, are answered by examining the historical facts.

While the *BNA Act* is "law," its enactment and the words it contains are "facts." The assumptions made by the Fathers of Confederation which explain why those words were used in the *BNA Act* are also facts. If instead of the nature and role of the Senate, the question is the nature and extent of the Federal government's "spending power" and whether it extends to F.P.F.T., the answer to the legal question will be determined by exactly the same process. By examining the relevant historical facts. No matter how "inconvenient" the provisions of the Constitution may

---

18 Senate *Reference* para. 25.

now be perceived by some to be in 2015, or how difficult it may be to amend those allegedly "inconvenient" provisions, the Constitution is the Constitution and must be implemented as written. The Court's duty is to enforce the law, not to change it.

So we must look at the historical record concerning the nature and scope of the Federal government's "spending power", with a view to discerning the "structure of government," (that the *BNA Act*) seeks to implement, (and) the assumptions made by the Fathers that underlie the "text" to see whether or not the federal spending power includes or excludes F.P.F.T..

The historical records that the Supreme Court consulted in the Quebec Separation case, and the two senate reference cases, are now conveniently collected in G. P. Browne's *Documents on the Confederation of British North America* (2009).[19]

The first document of interest is Browne's book,[20] is document 17, written on January 27, 1860 by the Duke of Newcastle, the Colonial Secretary in the British Cabinet, as a "circular dispatch."

It states that:

> *"Her Majesty's (Queen Victoria's) Government sees no reason to depart from the general line of policy which they have hitherto pronounced it is their intention to adopt if the occasion should arise. They do not think it their duty to initiate any movement towards such union [i.e. "a federal union of the British North American provinces;], but they have no wish to impede any well considered scheme which may have the concurrence of the people of the provinces through their legislatures, assuming of course that it does not interfere with Imperial interests."*

With this statement in mind the Fathers of Confederation, all of whom were representatives of those British North American Provinces, gathered at Quebec City on October 10, 1864 to consider, and if possible, to agree to a *"federal union"* of their Provinces. All of the Fathers were well aware that the scheme agreed to would have to define the terms of

---

19 *Carleton Library Series* 215, McGill — Queen's University Press (2009).
20 Browne Documents p. 30.

the union in "*its Constitution*," and that the resulting agreement would have to be implemented by a British statute.

The delegates to the Quebec Conference included many well-known figures of Canadian history. The Province of Canada, which had, by British statute, been created in 1840 by the union of the former Provinces of Upper Canada (now Ontario) and Lower Canada (now Quebec), was represented by (among others), John Alexander Macdonald (who became the first Prime Minister of the new country), by George Brown MAPP. the President of its Executive Council (and the founder of the newspaper which became the *Globe & Mail*), Sir E. P. Táche, Receiver-General and Alexander Galt its Minister of Finance.

On the first day of the conference John A. Macdonald put the following motion to the delegates:

> "*That the best interests and present and future prosperity of British North America will be promoted by a federal union under the Crown of Great Britain provided such union can be effected on principles just to the several provinces.*"

The motion was unanimously adopted by the delegates and became Quebec Resolution No. 1.

In speaking to this resolution Macdonald made specific reference to the fact that the interests of the Fathers' Provinces would be protected by British Judges. Macdonald was a lawyer and would have known that it was the Judges of the Privy Council that would afford that protection. This is what he said:

> "*The people of every Section (province) must feel that they are protected, and by no overstraining of central authority should such guarantees be overridden. Our constitution must be based on an Act of the Imperial Parliament, and any question as to overriding Sectional matters determined by "is it legal or not?" The judicial tribunals of Great Britain would settle any such difficulties should they occur.*"[21]

On Wednesday, October 12 the delegates agreed to the new union's

---

21 Document 32, Browne, page 95.

governmental structure. They began by adopting a motion proposed by George Brown, stating that:

> "In the Federation of the British North American provinces the system of government best adapted under existing circumstances to protect the diversified interests of the several provinces, and secure efficiency, harmony, and permanency in the working of the Union, — would be a General government charged with matters of common interest to the whole country, and Local governments for each of the Canada's and for the provinces of Nova Scotia, New Brunswick, and Prince Edward Island, charged with the control of local matters in their respective Sections, provision being made for the admission into the Union on equitable terms of Newfoundland, the Northwest Territory, British Columbia and Vancouver."[22]

That resolution became Quebec Resolution No. 2.

There can be no doubt that the Fathers intended that the governmental authority to be exercised by the General (Federal) government was to be different than the governmental authority to be exercised by the local (Provincial) governments. The Fathers were well aware that the powers that were to be conferred on the new general government would be powers their Provincial governments had exercised in the past and were exercising in October 1864. They knew that the powers that were to be conferred on the new General government would no longer be exercisable by their Provincial governments should confederation become a reality, but they did not want to give up the provincial powers necessary to "control local matters."

On the next day (October 13, 1864) the Conference adopted this motion:

> "That in framing a Constitution for the General Government, the Conference, with a view to the perpetuation of our connection with the Mother Country, and to the promotion of the best interests of the people of these provinces, desire to follow the model of the British Constitution, so far as our circumstances will permit."[23]

That became Quebec Resolution No. 3 and a part of the first recital

---

22 Document 31, Browne (pp. 62 and 154).
23 Browne Documents page 63.

to the *BNA Act*, so that, in addition to the explicit provisions of the *BNA Act*, the principles of the British Constitution would apply in Canada. One of these principles is the principle of "legality" (otherwise known as "the Rule of Law[24]").

In his book Democratic Government and Politics, Queen's University Professor J.A. Corry (1899-1985) explains what "Constitutionalism" means:

Rule By Law and Constitutionalism

"Closely related to the ideal of rule by law is the ideal of constitutionalism. Starting from the conviction that government action should be in accordance with law carefully laid down beforehand, it holds that the best way to accomplish this is to establish a fundamental law which defines the organs of government, prescribes how they shall function, and outlines the basic relationships between government and the private citizen. Government is then denied the power to change this fundamental law and required to observe its terms. Actually, of course, constitutionalism is a means for achieving the ideal of rule by law. But in the democratic world, the constitution has become a symbol around which men who are in disagreement on other points can be rallied. A special sanctity attaches to the constitution, and a special revulsion to unconstitutional actions or proposals."

The principle of legality also includes the ancient rule laid down in the case of *Entick* v. *Carrington* (1765) that *"the fact of a continued undisputed exercise of a power by a public body is immaterial, unless it points to a customary power exercised from time immemorial."*[25] Consequently, even if the Federal government had begun to make unauthorized F.P.F.T. on July 1, 1867 they would have been then (and would remain) illegal unless and until authorized by an amendment to the *BNA Act*. Consequently, the Federal government's purported use of a supposed but non-existent power could not and did not create it.

---

24 8(2) Hals, 4th, Para. 6.

25 Time immemorial is no later than 1688, the date of the Bill of Rights created as a result of the "glorious revolution" which deposed the Catholic James II and replaced him with the Protestant William of Orange. Needless to say, F.P.F.T. do not date back to "time immemorial."

Quebec Resolution 1 as well as Resolution 3 became part of the first recital to the *BNA Act*.[26]

Resolution No. 2 made it necessary for the Fathers to define as precisely as possible "*matters of common interest to the whole country*" in order to clothe the new general Parliament with the powers appropriate to its role as the government of the "whole country" leaving the provincial Parliaments with the powers appropriate to the control of "local matters."

We can now come directly to the F.P.F.T. question.

This is the record for Friday, October 21st:

"Friday, 21st October 1864.

The Chairman took the chair at ten o'clock a.m., when the members were convened.

It was moved by the Honourable Mr. John A. Macdonald: —

That it shall be competent for the General Legislature to make laws for the peace, welfare and good government of the Federated provinces (saving the sovereignty of England), and especially laws respecting: —

1. *Trade and commerce.*

2. *The imposition or regulation of duties of customs on imports and exports.*

3. *The imposition or regulation of excise duties.*

4. *All or any other modes or systems of taxation.*[27]

---

26 This recital is; "*Whereas the Provinces of Canada, Nova Scotia, and New Brunswick have expressed their desire to be federally united into One Dominion under the Crown of the United Kingdom of Great Britain and Ireland, with a Constitution similar in Principle to that of the United Kingdom.*"

27 When the Quebec Conference was convened in 1864 the Provinces in British North America maintained themselves by the imposition of import and excise taxes (e.g. Sales taxes) which were known as indirect taxes. They were indirect because they were basically hidden in the prices paid for the goods subject to that taxation. Direct taxes on the other hand are, like income taxes, imposed upon and collected directly from the taxpayer liable for them who could not but be aware of the burden. Real property taxes which are typically imposed on the owners of the taxed

5. Currency and coinage.

6. The borrowing of money on the public credit.

7. Banking and the issue of paper money.

8. The law relating to bills of exchange and promissory notes.

9. The rate of interest.

10. Legal tender.

11. Weights and measures.

12. Postal service

13. Bankruptcy and insolvent laws operating as a discharge of the debtor.

14. Beacons and lighthouses.

15. Ocean navigation and shipping.

16. Sea fisheries.

17. Patents of invention and discovery.

18. Copy Rights.

19. Telegraphic communication and the incorporation of telegraph companies.

20. Naturalization.

21. Marriage and divorce.

22. The taking of the census.

23. Militia — Military and naval service and defence.

24. Immigration.

25. Agriculture.

26. The criminal law (except the constitution of Courts of Criminal Jurisdiction).

27. Roads, bridges, lines of steam or other ships, railways, canals

---

property are also open (not hidden) and are also direct taxes. It was thought at the time that direct taxes were extremely unpopular and for reasons best known to the Fathers, the Quebec Resolutions and the *BNA Act* gave the Federal government the authority to impose both direct and indirect taxation but confined the Provinces to the imposition of direct taxes only.

(The Allocation of Taxing Power Under the Canadian Constitution, 2d Ed,. G.V. LaForest — The Canadian Tax Foundation (1982)).

and other works connecting any two or more of the provinces together or extending beyond the limits of any one Province.

28. *All such works as shall, although lying wholly within any one Province, be specially declared by the Acts authorizing them to be for the general advantage.*

29. *The establishment of a general Court of Appeal for the Federated Provinces.*

30. *Subsidies or grants in aid of the Local Governments.*

31. *The public debt and public property.*

32. *And generally respecting all matters of a general character, not specially and exclusively reserved for the Local governments and legislatures."*[28]

If this motion had been adopted then item 30 (F.P.F.T.) would have been included in the list of subjects "respecting" which the General legislature was to be competent "*to make laws,*" and "*Federal/Provincial fiscal transfers*" would have been made constitutional. However, the motion in the form put to the conference by Macdonald *was not adopted. It was rejected!*

The record for October 21, 1864 continues:

"And after further debate, —

And the adoption by the Honourable Mr. John A. Macdonald of certain amendments to his motion, the question of concurrence was put thereon, and then was resolved in the affirmative as follows: —

That it shall be competent for the General Legislature to make laws for the peace, welfare and good government of the Federated provinces (saving the sovereignty of England), and especially laws respecting: —

1. *Trade and commerce.*

2. *The imposition or regulation of duties of Customs on imports and exports.*

3. *The imposition or regulation of excise duties.*

---

28 Browne Documents pp. 76-77.

4. All or any other modes or systems of taxation.

5. Currency and coinage.

6. The borrowing of money on the public credit.

7. Banking and the issue of paper money.

8. The law relating to bills of exchange and promissory notes.

9. Interest.

10. Legal tender.

11. Weights and measures.

12. Postal service.

13. Bankruptcy and insolvency.

14. Beacons, buoys and lighthouses.

15. Navigation and shipping.

16. Sea fisheries.

17. Patents of invention and discovery.

18. Copy Rights.

19. Telegraphic communication and the incorporation of telegraph companies.

20. Naturalization and aliens.

21. Marriage and divorce.

22. The census.

23. Militia — Military and naval service and defence.

24. Immigration.

25. Agriculture,

26. The Criminal law (except the constitution of Courts of Criminal Jurisdiction).

27. Lines of steamships or other ships, railways and canals connecting any two or more of the provinces together.

28. Lines of steamships between the Federated provinces and other countries.

And at the hour of half-past four o'clock p.m., a motion for

> *adjournment being carried, the Chairman declared the Conference continued until to-morrow at twelve o'clock noon."* [29]

Items 1 to 28 is the list of federal powers the Fathers finally adopted. **Item 30 in the original motion is conspicuously absent from Resolution 29 and from section 91 of the** *BNA Act.*

The records collected in Browne's book do not include the language of the amendments to the list of federal powers originally proposed by Macdonald, but it is abundantly clear from other sources why the Fathers rejected F.P.F.T.. George Brown disclosed the reason in his speech to the legislature of the Province of Canada on February 8, 1865 which I will come to shortly.

I have set out Macdonald's motion of October 21, 1864, both before and after its amendment, verbatim, to demonstrate that the Fathers consciously and deliberately decided that Parliament would not be given the power Macdonald had suggested it should have. This is part 1 of the F.P.F.T. story. Part 2 is as follows.

On Saturday October 22, 1864 the Fathers discussed how to deal with the property and other assets of the existing Provinces, and the question of whether and to what extent the new central government should be liable after Confederation for the debts that these Provinces had incurred. It is important to recall that items 2, 3 and 4 of the list of Federal powers adopted by the conference the day before included the power to impose duties and excise taxes (items 2 and 3) and to employ *"all or any other modes or systems of taxation"* (item 4).

On October 22, Alexander Galt moved that the new central government should have the ownership of those items of Provincial property specified in his motion and that the new central government would be responsible for all provincial debts up to specified dollar limits. Item 5 of Galt's motion then proposed that the Constitution should contain this provision:

> *"5. In consideration of the transfer to the General Legislature of the powers of taxation, a grant in aid of each Province shall be made, equal to an amount of 80 cents per head of the population, as established by the census of 1861; Newfoundland being estimated*

---

29 Browne Documents pp. 78-79.

> at 130,000 inhabitants. Such aid to be in full settlement of all future demands upon the General Legislature for local purposes, and to be payable half yearly in advance to each Province."[30]

Galt's motion was adopted on Wednesday, October 26th. Item 5 became Quebec Resolution 64 and thereafter section 118 of the *BNA Act*.

It is therefore indisputable that the framers of our Constitution decided in October 1864 that the Federal parliament's authority to make F.P.F.T. would be *limited* to the "grant(s) in aid" that were required to be made by Quebec Resolution 64 and section 118.

Consequently, the assumption which underlies the text of the *BNA Act* is indisputable. Parliament was not to possess any authority whatever to make any F.P.F.T. except for those required to be made by section 118. In other words, Parliament would not have any authority to make any other grants to the Provinces beyond the grants the Constitution required it to make.

The subject of Federal subsidies or transfers to the Provinces was never again discussed at Quebec. It was not discussed at the subsequent London Conference in December 1866 and it is not mentioned in any draft of the *BNA Act*, or in the *BNA Act*'s final text, except for section 118. As provided for in Galt's motion, section 118 requires the Federal government to pay, as a matter of constitutional obligation, not discretion, yearly grants to every province in stipulated and thereby fixed amounts. While those fixed amounts may have seemed significant in 1864, they are no more than rounding errors in the Federal accounts today. But it matters not whether the amounts the Federal government was required to pay by reason of section 118 are large or small. *What matters is that the Fathers of Confederation consciously and deliberately decided that the Federal government would not have the constitutional authority to use federal public money to subsidize any Provincial government at any time, for any reason, with the exception of the payments required by section 118*,[31] and some miscellaneous and long obsolete

---

30 Browne Documents. pp. 79-81.
31 Section 118 was replaced by the *British North America Act*, 1907 which increased the mandatory subsidies somewhat. They have not been changed since.

payments related to the pre-confederation debts of Nova Scotia and New Brunswick as provided for in Resolutions 63 and 65.

The list of Provincial powers, as defined by the Fathers of Confederation, became Quebec Resolution 43 and then section 92 of the *BNA Act*. Sections 91 and 92 declare that the lists of Federal and Provincial powers are mutually exclusive, which is why the Privy Council described those powers as being contained in separate and "watertight compartments,"[32] a characterization approved of by the Chief Justice of Canada in the 1981 reference concerning the resolution to seek the enactment of the *Constitution Act, 1982*.[33] In that case, Chief Justice Laskin said, on behalf of the majority of the Supreme Court referring to whether the *BNA Act* could be amended by the British Parliament without the Provinces' consent, said:

> *"History cannot alter the fact there is a British statute to construe and apply in relation to a matter, fundamental as it is, that is not provided for by the statute."*

Consequently, the ordinary rules of statutory interpretation govern the interpretation of the *BNA Act*. There are no other rules.

The subject matters listed in sections 91 and 92 of the *BNA Act* are known as "heads" of power. By section 91, Parliament is authorized to make laws "in relation to" the heads of power listed in section 91, while the provincial legislatures are authorized to make laws "in relation to" the provincial heads of power listed in section 92.

In most cases, the two mutually exclusive lists of federal and provincial heads of power is sufficient to determine whether any particular law is within one list or the other. The task is not always easy but is eventually resolved by a court deciding whether a challenged law is or is not in "pith and substance" within heads of power assigned by the constitution to the legislative body which enacted it.

However, the contrast between the federal taxing power as expressed in section 91(3), and the provincial taxing power as expressed in section 92(2), gave rise to a problem. Section 92(2) limits provincial taxes to direct taxes imposed to raise revenues "for provincial purpose" while

---

32 *A.G. v. A.G. Ont.*, [1937] A.C. 326 at 354.
33 *Re: Resolution to amend the Constitution*, [1981] 1 S.C.R. 753 at 788.

the federal taxing power, which might have said that it was limited to taxation intended to raise revenues for "federal purposes," did not expressly say so. The Privy Council eventually held that the federal taxation power was limited to the imposition of taxes for federal purposes and Parliament was constitutionally prohibited from raising any money by taxation for "provincial purposes." That determination was made in 1932, in the *Insurance Act* case.[34] In light of sections 102 and 126 of the *BNA Act* that was the only possible conclusion the Privy Council could have come to.

In the same year, the Privy Council was required to decide whether a debt owed to the Federal government (The Crown in Right of Canada) took precedence in the bankruptcy of Silver Brothers Ltd., over the claim of the government of Quebec (The Crown in Right of the Province of Quebec). According to both federal and provincial legislation, debts owing to the Crown took precedence over other debts in the case of bankruptcy of the debtor.

Both debts were in respect of taxes, and it was argued that when federal and provincial legislation came into conflict the doctrine of "paramountcy" required that the federal claim prevailed over the provincial claim. The Privy Council held that the doctrine of paramountcy did not apply in those circumstances. The federal and provincial tax legislation were not in conflict as the two taxations (could) stand side by side without interfering with each other so that the claims of both governments were equal. As the bankrupt estate was without sufficient assets to satisfy both claims, the federal and Provincial governments were obliged to share in the assets of *Silver Brothers* that were available, equally.

The Privy Council put it this way:

> "It is true that there is only one Crown, but as regards Crown revenues and Crown property by legislation assented to by the Crown there is a distinction made between the revenues and property in the Province and the revenues and property in the Dominion. There are two separate statutory purses. In each the ingathering and expending authority is different."[35]

---

34 In *Re: The Insurance Act of Canada*, [1932] A.C. 41.
35 In *re: Silver Brothers Limited*, [1932] A.C. 514 at 524.

And so, the Federal government's purse is completely separate from the Provincial governments' purses and the "ingathering" (taxation) and "expending" (spending) authority is different. *Consequently, neither the Federal government nor any Provincial government may "ingather" any money to augment the others purse, as had been held three months earlier in the Insurance Act case.*[36]

The *Insurance Act* case (*In re: The Insurance Act of Canada*) concerned an attempt by Parliament to require an Insurance company licensed to carry on business under the *Quebec Insurance Act* to also obtain a licence under *The Insurance Act of Canada*. The Privy Council had held in 1991 in the *Person's* case[37] that the regulation of insurance contracts was within the legislative jurisdiction of the Provinces and beyond the legislative jurisdiction of the Parliament of the Dominion.

It is therefore clear that the separate purses and watertight compartments are essential ingredients of the "original contract upon which the (Canadian) federation was founded" and cannot be changed by judicial interpretation as the Supreme Court made clear in the *Upper House* case in quoting from the judgment of the Privy Council in the *Aeronautics* case.

The Privy Council's decisions in *Silver Brothers* and the *Insurance Act* cases in the 1930's were entirely predictable by anyone who had read that Court's judgment in the *Maritime Bank* case of 1892.[38] In that case, the Privy Council was required to decide whether the governmental powers exercisable by the federal and Provincial governments under the common law (Royal Prerogative powers) were divided between Parliament on the one hand, and the provincial legislatures on the other. The Federal government had argued in that case that it was entitled to exercise those powers and the provincial legislatures were not.

This is how the Privy Council decided that question in 1892:

> *"Their Lordships do not think it necessary to examine, in minute detail the provisions of the Act of 1867, which nowhere profess to curtail in any respect the rights and privileges of the Crown,*

---

36 [1932] A.C. 41.
37 *The Citizens Insurance Company v. Parsons* (1881-1882), 7 A.C. 96.
38 *Liquidators of the Maritime Bank of Canada v. Receiver-General of New Brunswick*, [1892] A.C. 437.

> or to disturb the relations then subsisting between the Sovereign and the provinces. The object of the Act was neither to weld the provinces into one, nor to subordinate Provincial governments to a central authority, but to create a Federal government in which they should all be represented, entrusted with the exclusive administration of affairs in which they had a common interest, each province retaining its independence and autonomy. That object was accomplished by distributing, between the Dominion and the provinces, all powers executive and legislative, and all public property and revenues which had previously belonged to the provinces; so that the Dominion Government should be vested with such of these powers, property, and revenues as were necessary for the due performance of its constitutional functions, and that the remainder should be retained by the provinces for the purposes of Provincial government."

Thus, the *BNA Act* divides *all* governmental powers between Ottawa and the Provinces. "*All*" must include both the power to impose taxation and the power to spend the proceeds.

It is also worth repeating here, the Supreme Court's statement in the 2014 *Senate Reference* case that:

> "The Constitution must be interpreted with a view to discerning the structure of government it seeks to implement."

This is a rule of statutory interpretation which was enunciated by Chief Justice Sir Edward Coke almost four hundred years ago in his *Institutes of The Laws of England* in which he said that the duty of any Court charged with the task of determining the meaning of a statute to interpret it *"according to the intent of them that made it.":*

"Them that made" the *BNA Act* were clearly the Fathers of Confederation.

Sir Edward Coke (pronounced Cook, 1552-1634) was an English barrister, a Member of Parliament and Chief Justice of England. He was the author of "The Institutes of the Laws of England" which were contained in four books published from 1628 to 1644 quoted by English judges from that day to this. For example, Viscount Dilhorne a judge of what was then the English House of Lords (the highest court of

Appeal in England) had this to say in *Stock v. Frank Jones (Tipton Ltd.)*[39] concerning the proper way to interpret statues:

> *"It is now fashionable to talk of a purposive construction of a statute, but it has been recognised since the 17th century that it is the task of the judiciary in interpreting an Act to seek to interpret it, according to intent of them that made it."* [40]

If it were the case that it appeared that an Act might have been better drafted, or that amendment to it might be less productive of anomalies, it is not open to the Court to remedy the defect. That must be left to the legislature. This rule applies of course to the *BNA Act*, the *Canadian Constitution* which as the Supreme Court of Canada said in the *Senate Reference* case:

> *"must be interpreted with a view to discerning the structure of government it seeks to implement."*

It is therefore beyond any doubt or the possibility of any argument that "them that made" the *BNA Act* deliberately rejected Macdonald's motion of October 24, 1864 concerning F.P.F.T. and the British Parliament implemented that decision by denying Parliament the right to take any money from any federal taxpayer in order to fund any Provincial government.

Whether the separate purses or the watertight compartment metaphors are employed, both prohibit F.P.F.T.. That is the structure that the Fathers of Confederation agreed to that the *BNA Act* implements and the structure which prohibits F.P.F.T..

The Federal Government may lawfully make gifts of its public money if and only if the expenditure is necessarily incidental to a law made by Parliament *in relation* to a subject matter specifically listed in section 91. For example, Parliament can and does provide a great deal of money to Indians because: "Indians and bands reserved for the Indians is a head of Federal power by reason of section 91(24). But "subsidies or grants in aid" of the Provinces, do not appear in section 91 or anywhere else in the *BNA Act*, except for section 118 and no such words have been added

---

39 (1918) 1 W.L.R. 231 at 234.
40 Coke 4. Inst. 330.

to the *BNA Act* since 1867. Consequently, the spending of federal public money to fund F.P.F.T. is not a head of federal power and is therefore prohibited.

In the light of this indisputable history, it is quite irrational to assert that the Federal Government has ever possessed the power to make F.P.F.T. or to spend its taxpayers' money for any purpose whatsoever other than purposes related to Parliament's constitutional authority to make laws "in relation to ... matters coming within the classes of subjects ... enumerated" in section 91, or specifically provided for in some other section of the *BNA Act* such as section 94A (Old Age Pensions), or to discharge its obligations originally required by section 118 and since 1907, by *The British North America Act 1907*.

The Quebec Conference concluded with the adoption of 72 formal resolutions set forth in a report to the Governor General dated November 7, 1864.[41] Thereafter, the delegates to the conference returned to their respective Provinces to seek their approval by their Provincial governments.

The resolutions were taken up again in London, England on December 4, 1866 and after revisions become 69 resolutions that were sent to Lord Carnarvon, the British Colonial Secretary by Macdonald on December 26th, 1866. The first draft of the *BNA Act* seems to have been prepared in January 1867. The final draft is dated February 9, 1867.[42]

The final draft became a Bill that was submitted to the Parliament at Westminster in February. It was enacted and received Queen Victoria's assent on March 29, 1867 and proclaimed in force as of July 1, 1867.

On February 8, 1865 in the legislature of the Province of Canada, George Brown explained his objections to the system that had existed as a result of the Act of the Union of 1840, uniting the former Provinces of Upper and Lower Canada, and how the agreement reached at Quebec would remove those objections:

> "We have also complained that immense sums of public money have been systematically taken from the public chest for local purposes of Lower Canada, in which the people of Upper Canada

---

41 Browne Documents, 34 and 40.
42 Browne Documents, 73, 78 and 86.

had no interest whatever, though compelled to contribute three-fourths of the cash. Well, sir, this scheme remedies that. All local matters are to be banished from the general legislature; local governments are to have control over local affairs, and if our friends in Lower Canada choose to be extravagant, they will have to bear the burden of it themselves. (hear hear) ..." [43]

Brown's remarks were the product of his own experience after Upper and Lower Canada had been united in 1840. In the light of the Federal government's abuse of power and interminable disputes we have seen in this country over the Provinces' supposed entitlement to "fair shares" of Federal taxpayers' money, through F.P.F.T. the Fathers of Confederation must be turning over in their graves.

Canada is a democracy and as a constitutional monarchy it was fashioned by the Fathers of Confederation with a Constitution similar in principle to that of the United Kingdom. As such, it is the Federal and Provincial Parliaments that are entitled to make laws, which is to say to transform policies into law in the form of statutes. Neither the monarch nor the courts (composed of non-elected judges) have any right whatsoever to make, amend or repeal any such laws in order to promote their own policy preferences.

As the then Lord Chancellor (Earl Loreburn) said on behalf of the Privy Council in the 1912 *"Companies Reference"*[44] case.

> *"It is true that from time to time the Courts of this and of other countries, whether under the British flag or not, have to consider and set aside as void, transactions upon the ground that they are against public policy. But no such doctrine can apply to an Act of Parliament. It is applicable only to the transactions of individuals. It cannot be too strongly put that with the wisdom or expediency or policy of an Act, lawfully passed no Court has a word to say."*

In 2010, the Federal government asked the Supreme Court to consider whether or not a proposed federal "Securities Act" (which would have set up a single National Securities regulator to replace

---

43 *Canada's Founding Debates*, Ajzenstat, Romney, Gentles and Gairdner, University of Toronto Press, p. 288.
44 [1912] A.C. 571 at 583.

provincial bodies such as the Ontario Securities Commission), was within the Constitutional authority of Parliament to enact, the Supreme Court of Canada decided, unanimously, that it was not. In paragraph 10 of its judgment the Court said:

> "While the parties presented evidence and arguments on the relative merits of federal and provincial regulation of securities, the policy question of whether a Single National Security Scheme is preferable to multiple provincial regimes is not one for the courts to decide. Accordingly, our answer to the reference question is dictated solely by the text of the Constitution, fundamental constitutional principles and the relevant case law."[45]

The "relevant case law," referred to by the Supreme Court in the *Securities* reference includes the judgment of the Privy Council in *Citizens Insurance of Canada v. Parsons* decided in 1881,[46] which contained the first and still leading statement of the scope of the (federal) trade and commerce power, and which held that that federal power did not "include the power to regulate the contracts of a particular business or trade in a province." In *Parsons* the trade was the sale of fire insurance policies, in the *Securities Act* case it was contracts for the sale of securities.

After the conclusion of the Quebec conference, the governments of PEI and Newfoundland chose not to join the union, but the Quebec resolutions were agreed to by the Provinces of Canada (now Ontario and Quebec); Nova Scotia and New Brunswick and their delegates attended a subsequent conference held in London in December 1866. The London Conference adopted 69 Resolutions, which for all practical purposes were the same resolutions as those adopted at Quebec. PEI eventually joined the union in 1873 and Newfoundland in 1949, but I very much doubt that either province did so with the expectation that their residents would be forced (through federal taxes) to fund the construction of municipal transportation facilities by the TTC (Toronto Transit Commission), which they now must do as a result of F.P.F.T..

It is difficult to imagine that the funding of a municipal subway system anywhere in Canada is a matter of "common interest to the

---

45 2011 S.C. 66 at para. 10.
46 (1881), 7 App-Case 6.

whole country" rather than a "local matter" and cannot possibly be a matter of interest to every federal taxpayer in every area of the country. Section 92(8) of the *BNA Act* has, from July 1, 1867 to date, given the exclusive authority to make laws in relation to "municipal institutions" in the province to the provincial legislatures. Parliament has never had any authority whatsoever to give federal taxpayers money to any city, town or village but has regularly done so, and continues to do so.

There are two further Quebec Resolutions that should be mentioned as they reflected centuries old principles of English (and therefore) Canadian constitutional law.

Resolution 48 provided that "*all bills for appropriating any part of the public revenue, or for imposing any new tax ... shall originate in the House of Commons or the House of Assembly (of a province) as the case may be.*"

Resolution 49 prohibited either Parliament or a Provincial legislature from introducing or enacting any Bill to authorize any appropriation (i.e. spending) or the imposition of any tax unless the purpose of the proposed appropriation or the proposed tax was "*first recommended (to the relevant legislature) by message of the Governor General (or the Lieutenant Governor of the relevant province).*"

These resolutions became sections 53 and 54 of the *BNA Act*[47] and reflect the constitutional principle that only a Parliament (the peoples' representatives) can authorize taxation or the spending of the State's money, which dates back to *Magna Carta*. King George III's violation of that principle led to the Boston Tea Party and the American Revolution.

The Privy Council's description of the *BNA Act*'s division of federal and provincial revenues into two separate purses is completely accurate as that is exactly what sections 102 and 126 of the *BNA Act* provide for. In the context of sections 102 and 126, the "Public Service of Canada" is distinguished from the "Public Service" of a province and in each case the spending (appropriation) authorized by those sections is limited to the one or the other. It follows as night follows day that no federal revenue whatever may lawfully be appropriated for the public service of a province except to meet its obligations to make the payments to the province required by the *Constitution Act, 1907*.

---

47 By section 90 of the *BNA Act* these Sections are made applicable to the provincial legislature.

Accordingly, any money provided to a province by F.P.F.T. can only be spent by the recipient for the public service of that province. It is therefore beyond all doubt that there cannot be any transfer of any money taken from the Consolidated Revenue Fund of Canada to a province other than money taken to honour the Federal government's Constitutional obligations under the *British North America Act 1907*.

As will be seen some of those who assert that (despite the history and the explicit provisions of the *BNA Act*) federal transfers are constitutional argue that some words (which are never specified) should be "read into" the *BNA Act* so as to treat the *BNA Act* as if it contained the provision (suggested by Macdonald) which the Fathers of Confederation refused to include.

In the Introduction, I referenced A.P. Herbert's Lord Mildew and his witty statement of the cardinal rule of statutory interpretation, "if Parliament does not mean what it says it must say so."

In the words of a modern and **real** law lord:

> *"It is a strong thing to read into an Act of Parliament words which are not there, and in the absence of clear necessity it is a wrong thing to do."* [48]

The Fathers of Confederation were able to and entitled to consider including, in what became section 91 of the *BNA Act*, "subsidies or grants in aid" of the Provinces, as a head of Federal power. They were also entitled to decide against giving Parliament that power. Likewise the British Parliament was able, some years after enacting the *BNA Act* to create Australia as a commonwealth of the "states" of New South Wales, Victoria, South Australia, Queensland, Tasmania and Western Australia upon the terms that Queen Victoria said: "we are satisfied that the people of Australia have agreed (to)." In contrast to the *BNA Act*, the Constitution of Australia includes the following as section 96:

> **"96 Financial assistance to States**
>
> *During a period of ten years after the establishment of the Commonwealth and thereafter until the Parliament otherwise*

---

[48] Lord Bridge of Harwich in *Steele Ford and Newton* v. Crown Prosecution Service[1994] 1 A.C. 22 at 33.

provides, the Parliament may grant financial assistance to any State on such terms and conditions as the Parliament thinks fit." [49]

The people of Australia obviously decided that their federal Parliament should have the constitutional authority to make F.P.F.T. payments and so it *does*. The wishes of the Canadians (expressed by the Fathers of Confederation) was that the Canadian Parliament should not have that power and so *it doesn't*.

Anyone who can explain how the BNA Act can be read as if it included the words suggested by Sir John A. Macdonald on October 21, 1864 or their equivalent (such as section 96 of the Australian Constitution) is free to try and some have.

Can it be that the lawyers, law professors, judges and others who have expressed the opinion that F.P.F.T. are constitutional are entirely ignorant of the proceedings of the Quebec Conference? It certainly seems so.

---

49 *Commonwealth of Australia Constitution Act*, enacted July 9, 1900, in force January 1, 1901.

CHAPTER 3

The History of Federal/Provincial Transfer Payments

When the *BNA Act* was proclaimed in force as of July 1, 1867, section 118 required Canada to pay "yearly" to the Provinces "for the support of their Governments and legislatures" specified fixed amounts and "an annual grant in Aid of each Province ... equal to Eighty Cents Per Head of the Population..." and stated that "Such Grants shall be in full settlement of all future Demands on Canada."

Yet on June 22nd 1869, less than two years after the *BNA Act* came into force, the federal Parliament under Prime Minister John A. Macdonald enacted a statute providing for additional transfer payments to Nova Scotia.[50] This statute was the work of the gentleman who had proposed on October 21, 1864 that Parliament be authorized to make transfer payments to the Provinces whenever it chose to and in any amounts it chose to — a proposal which was rejected and replaced by section 118.

The last section of this 1869 statute stated that:

> "The grants and provisions made by this Act, and the British North America Act 1867 shall be in full settlement of all demands on Canada by Nova Scotia."

---

50 An Act respecting Nova Scotia 1869 32-33 Vict. C.2.

Macdonald was a lawyer and was thoroughly familiar with the decisions the Fathers had made at Quebec, and the provisions of section 118 of the *BNA Act*. He could not possibly have thought that the *Nova Scotia Act* was anything but *ultra vires*. Macdonald does not deserve to be thought of as a great Prime Minister unless the willingness to abuse political power is the criterion to be used to determine that status.

According to Dr. O.D. Skelton (who had succeeded Sir Joseph Pope as Under-Secretary of state), the leader of the Liberal opposition (Edward Blake)[51] "moved in the House of Commons against Macdonald's *Nova Scotia Act* on the ground that it was an unauthorized assumption of power on the part of the Dominion. Not surprisingly, the Dominion Parliament, (led by Macdonald), declined to accept Blake's view and the law officers of the Crown in London, advised that the Act was one which the Dominion Parliament was competent to pass under section 91."[52]

The "opinion", such as it is, took the form of a joint letter from the British Attorney General and Solicitor General dated August 10, 1869[53] to Lord Granville (the Colonial Secretary) in London which simply stated:

> "We have the honour to report that we think the Act ... is one which under the 91st Section (of the BNA Act) it was within the competence of the Parliament of Canada to pass."

On August 23, 1869 Lord Granville wrote to Sir John Young the Governor General of Canada as follows:

> "As I observed that a doubt was entertained during the passing of the Act respecting Nova Scotia ... whether it was competent for the Legislature of Canada to pass such a measure I thought it desirable to take the opinion of the Law Officers of the Crown upon the point and I have been advised that the Act is one which it was competent for the Parliament of Canada to pass under the powers vested in it by the 91st Section of the British North America Act 1867."[54]

---

51 Edward Blake was one of the best lawyers Canada has ever produced.
52 British North America Acts and Selected Statutes 1867-1943, Queen's Printer 1943, Page 82, Note 62.
53 Public Records Office, Colonial Office.
54 National Archives, RG 7, G1, Vol. 175, pp 374-395.

There are no "reasons" whatever provided for in this "opinion" or in either of these letters, nor is there any trace of any memorandum or other record of the reasons (if any) for the "Law Officers" opinion in the archives in Ottawa or London (England).

Neither Macdonald's notes, nor the Minutes of the Quebec Conference were published until 1895, more than 20 years later. Accordingly, there was no way for the "law officers of the Crown in London to know in 1869, that the Fathers had deliberately denied Parliament the authority to enact the Nova Scotia statute." It also appears that the "law officers of the Crown" did not bother to read the *BNA Act* or they would have encountered sections 102, 118 and 126.

It is also apparent that the "law officers of the Crown" who are alleged to have provided this advice were also ignorant of the judgment of the privy council in the *Companies Reference* concerning how the *BNA Act* was to be interpreted, delivered over 40 years later, stating that:

> *"In the interpretation of a completely self-governing Constitution founded upon a written organic instrument, such as the British North America Act, if the text is explicit the text is conclusive, alike in what it directs and what it forbids."* [55]

What the *BNA Act* "directs" is the payments required by section 118. What it "forbids" is any other F.P.F.T..

Unfortunately, the 1869 *BNA Act* respecting Nova Scotia, although the first was not to be the last breach of the *BNA Act*. Dr. O.D. Skelton reported that:

> *"In the sixty years since 1869 (up to 1929) there have been three general (statutory) revisions scaling up the grants given to all of the provinces and more than a score of special revisions affecting every one. Despite heavy withdrawals from capital account ... the four original provinces in 1928-29 drew more than 3½ times as much from the federal treasury as had been promised in the BNA Act."* [56]

Dr. Skelton (1878-1941) was educated at Queen's University and the University of Chicago. In 1925 he was appointed as Canada's

---

55 (1912) A.C. 571 at 583.
56 OP Cit. p. 82.

under-secretary for foreign affairs. He was an adviser to two prime ministers, Wilfred Laurier and Mackenzie King. He was described by the C.B.C. as the most influential public servant in Canadian history.

In April 1907, the government of Sir Wilfred Laurier (who was clearly a more principled Prime Minister than Macdonald) petitioned King Edward VII, seeking a formal amendment to the *BNA Act* stating; "*that it is expedient to amend the scale of payments authorized under section 118 (of the BNA Act)*" and suggesting the amounts that should be substituted.

The British government acceded to the Laurier petition by enacting the *British North America Act, 1907* and thereby amending and replacing section 118.

All that can be said about the "Law Officers" of the British Crown as of 1869 is that their knowledge of the origins and content of the *BNA Act* was conspicuous by its absence.

It would appear that after the enactment of the *BNA Act 1907* in response to the Laurier petition, the Federal government adhered for some time to the requirements of the Constitution, but as Dr. Skelton noted that was not the case for very long. It is clear that by 1941 the Federal government's abuse of its constitutional authority concerning federal transfers had been resumed and was to accelerate in future years to monumental proportions.

During the Second World War, the Provinces agreed to refrain from imposing provincial income taxes so that the Federal government would have more "tax room" to raise the money, it said it required to fund Canada's war effort. In return the Provinces were to receive unconditional payments from the Federal government to compensate them for the lost revenue." However, after the war, when "war efforts" were no longer required, "the Federal government decided to maintain the wartime scheme in order to "finance peace time reconstruction and to use centralized fiscal policy as a tool of national economic management."[57]

There were, of course, no petitions to the British government seeking amendments to the *BNA Act* to authorize any increase in F.P.F.T. beyond those permitted by the 1907 amendment either for Canada's war efforts,

---

57 C.L.O.C. Section 6.3.

peace time reconstruction or to use F.P.F.T. as a tool for "national economic management."

While it is arguable that the circumstances of the war time years justified the Federal government's transfer payments as an authorized use of its emergency powers to make laws for the "Peace, Order and Good Government of Canada" under the opening words of section 91, that argument did not apply to justify spending for "reconstruction" or the use of "centralized fiscal policy" as a tool of "national economic management." Nevertheless, the transfer of federal tax-payers money to the Provinces to be spent for provincial (not federal purposes) has continued apace ever since.

In 1957 transfer payments to the Provinces included, for the first time, an "equalization payment" which was identified as such in the Federal Department of Finance's Accounts. The Public Accounts for 1958 show that "tax equalization payments," "provincial revenue stabilization payments" and "tax rental payments" were made to all 10 Provinces. All of these subsidies were "subsidies or grants in aid" of the Provinces, in John A. Macdonald's language and prohibited by the *BNA Act*.

By 1957 Louis St. Laurent, who had become a member of Mackenzie King's Cabinet during the war, became Prime Minister. As the record will show, he (like Macdonald) was well aware that his government had no authority whatever to give federal taxpayers money to the governments of the Provinces for any reason other than the need to honour its obligations under section 118 of the *BNA Act*, as amended in 1907. St. Laurent had acquired that knowledge as counsel for the Dominion in the *Insurance Act* case in 1932 and again in the *Unemployment Insurance Act* case of 1937.

In the *Unemployment Insurance Act* case, the question was whether or not a federal statute entitled "The Employment and Social Insurance Act" (enacted in 1935) was or was not within Parliament's Constitutional authority. That question was put to the Supreme Court of Canada in a reference.[58]

The *Employment and Social Insurance* Act was conceived by the government of R.B. Bennet as part of a Canadian "New Deal" adopted in

---

58 *In the matter of a Reference as to whether the Parliament of Canada had legislative jurisdiction to enact the Employment and Social Insurance Act,* [1936] S.C.R. 527.

imitation of President Roosevelt's program in the U.S.. Unfortunately for Bennet's political fortunes, his government was defeated by Mackenzie King's Liberals in October 1935. The King government referred the constitutionality of this "New Deal" legislation to the Supreme Court of Canada and retained two prominent lawyers to argue the Federal government's case, one from Ontario, (R.W. Rowell) and one from (Quebec, Louis St. Laurent).

Rowell and St. Laurent argued that the unemployment problem was nationwide and so serious a crisis as to be characterized as a national emergency. If the court had found that assertion to be correct, then the Federal government would have had the constitutional authority to enact the *Employment and Social Insurance Act* pursuant to Parliament's power found in the opening words of section 91(1), i.e. the power to "make laws for the Peace, Order and good Government of Canada in relation to all matters *not coming within the Classes of Subjects ... assigned exclusively to the Legislatures of the Provinces.*"

But, as the courts found, the *Employment and Social Insurance Act 1935* did not purport to address a National "Emergency." Instead it purported to establish a permanent system of compulsory Employment Insurance funded in part by mandatory contributions from employers and employees, and in part by money taken by parliament from the federal Consolidated Revenue Fund.

While the "emergency powers" argument was Plan A, St. Laurent had an alternative, Plan B, which was the argument that Parliament had the jurisdiction to enact the *Employment and Social Insurance Act* pursuant to:

"*its exclusive powers*

(a) to regulate trade and commerce,

(b) to raise money by any mode or system of taxation;

(c) to appropriate public money for any public purpose,

(d) to provide for the collection of statistics; and

(e) to enact criminal laws."[59]

---

59 Factum submitted on behalf of the Attorney General of Canada paragraph 9 (Supreme Court of Canada file). St. Laurent's Factum did not mention the sections

While the Supreme Court agreed that unemployment resulting from the great depression was certainly a problem throughout Canada, it could not be characterized as "an emergency amounting to a National peril." And so, the authority to "make laws for the Peace, Order and Good Government of Canada" under the opening words of section 91 of the *BNA Act* could not and did not authorize Parliament to enact the *Employment and Social Insurance Act, 1935*, as "emergency" legislation.

The Supreme Court also rejected the assertion that the legislation could be upheld as an exercise of the Federal government's taxing power following the judgment of the Privy Council in the 1932 *Insurance Act* case[60], or its right to legislate in relation to "The Public Debt and Property" under section 91(1) (now 91(1A)).

In the *Insurance Act* case, the Privy Council had decided that the federal taxation power was *limited* to the imposition of taxes to raise money to be spent for proper federal constitutional purposes which did not include legislation "in relation to" insurance. The Supreme Court observed (in the *Unemployment Insurance Act* case) that as unemployment was a provincial matter, Parliament could not use its powers of taxation to fund a scheme for alleviating its effects.

As the Privy Council had stated in the *Insurance Act* case:

> *"If it were otherwise the Parliament of Canada might in connection with any matter whatsoever, by the mere imposition of a tax, confer upon itself authority to legislate upon matters over which the legislature of each province would ordinarily have jurisdiction."*

St. Laurent's argument in the *Unemployment* case was the same argument the Privy Council had rejected in the *Insurance Act* case with federal "spending" substituted as the excuse, instead of "taxation."

It is therefore obvious that there cannot possibly be an *unlimited* federal "spending power" unless there is also and at the same time, an *unlimited* taxing power to support it. As the Fathers of Confederation had deleted federal transfers from what became section 91, Parliament was prohibited from imposing taxes to pay for them.

It must also be said that St. Laurent's argument (in the *Unemployment*

---

of the *BNA Act* by number.
60 In Re: *The Insurance Act of Canada*, [1932] A.C. 41.

case) deliberately misrepresented the Federal government's appropriation power. It is not and never was a power "to appropriate public money *for any public purpose.*" The power to appropriate money is limited by (section 102 of the *BNA Act*) to money required for the "Public Service of Canada." As F.P.F.T. can only be spent by the recipient Provinces for the public service of a province, it is not surprising that St. Laurent lost in the Supreme Court and lost again when he appealed to the Privy Council.

The judgment in the Supreme Court *had* not been unanimous. The dissenting judgment in the Supreme Court was authored by Chief Justice Duff, with one other judge (Davis, J.) agreeing with him.[61]

Unlike the majority, Duff accepted St. Laurent's argument that the Federal government's contribution to the Unemployment Insurance Fund was a valid exercise of Parliament's constitutional authority to make laws in relation to "The Public Debt and Property." Even so, Duff was still obliged to explain how federal tax revenues, even if they were properly characterized as "public property" once collected by the Federal government could be appropriated for a "provincial purpose," in the light of s. 102 of the *BNA Act*. Duff dealt with that obstacle by stating that Parliament of Canada (not the Court) had the unlimited discretion:

> "*To determine finally what objects are and what objects are not within the scope of the words "for the Public Service of Canada."*"

Duff's "interpretation" of section 102 would have made that section and section 126 entirely meaningless.

The Parliament which had the right to determine what objects are and what objects are not within the scope of the words "for the public service of Canada" was the British Parliament sitting at Westminster. It was that Parliament which enacted the *BNA Act*, and which divided legislative power between the Parliament of Canada and the provincial legislatures.

Duff, when sober, was considered to be an excellent lawyer but that

---

61 By 1941, when Duff delivered the unanimous judgment of the Supreme Court in Reference Re Section 16 of the Special *War Revenue Act*, [1942] S.C.R. 429 he had discovered the *Insurance Act* case and applied it.

was not the case while he was under the influence of the consumption of "strong drink."

His biographer (David Ricardo Williams) says this in "Duff — A Life in The Law" (page 82):

> "Duff may have been denied the Chief Justiceship of Canada in 1924 because of his drinking, and when R. B. Bennet finally gave him the promotion in 1933, he did so only after expressing serious reservations and extracting a pledge of good behavior."

In Mackenzie King's diary, he made this entry on September 12, 1924:

> "I have tried very hard to secure Lafleur as Chief Justice, but in vain. It leaves the choice between Duff & Anglin. The former is probably the abler but is dissipated, gets off on sprees for weeks at a time. Was intoxicated at last opening of Parliament and at Sir Louis Davies funeral. I regard him too as a bit of a sycophant where the Tories are concerned & more or less the favourite with the big interests. Anglin is narrow, has not a pleasant manner, is very vain, but industrious, steady and honest, a true liberal at heart. Both are personal friends. I imagine the bar as a whole prefer Duff, some do not know his habits ... Lapointe [the minister of justice] wishes to appoint Newcombe, the dep. Min. He will lose a good man & our friends will not like it, but it will please the Tories & will offset not appointing Duff .... While I wish we could have secured Lafleur& I do not altogether like appointing Anglin because of the feeling of the bar against him, I nevertheless think in the interests of justice and the dignity of the bench, his appointment is preferable to any other all circumstances considered."

Francis Alexander Anglin (1865-1933) was appointed Chief Justice of Canada on September 16, 1924 succeeding Sir Louis Davies.

Williams specifically mentions Duff's dissent in the *Unemployment Insurance* case stating that "his reasons are not convincing." After quotation parts of Duff's judgments, Williams said:

> "He strains for the decision. One wonders if his innate liberalism guided his pen, or if his admiration for Roosevelt and sympathy with Bennett's efforts to cure the country's economic ills might have influenced him. According to the late R.K. Finlayson, the

> *Conservative leader's executive secretary, Bennett used him during the court hearings as a messenger to take Duff explanations of the former government's legislative programme. Unwilling to intercede directly with the Chief Justice while the case was being argued, Bennett apparently had no compunction about using an intermediary to expound on his policies. Duff had once roundly condemned Mackenzie King for attempting to influence the court before the hearing of a far less important case. Bennett's intervention, and Duff's apparent willingness to listen, may be accounted for, if not excused, by the fact that the story was out of office and merely trying to shore up his self-esteem."*

It is grossly improper for any judge to communicate directly or indirectly with anyone interested in the outcome of any case he or she is hearing and must decide, other than his colleagues or office staff. There cannot be any doubt that Duff was well aware that this was so, yet he was communicating through intermediaries with the author of the *Employment and Social Insurance Act*. It is improper for any judge to engage in this conduct, but when the judge is the Chief Justice of Canada it is outrageous and ought to have resulted in his ouster from the bench.

Section 102 of the *BNA Act* is not meaningless, as the quotation from the *Silver Brothers* case (set forth earlier) clearly demonstrates. Canada's highest appellate court had decided, in 1932, that the *BNA Act* made a distinction "between the revenues and property in the Province and the revenues and property in the Dominion." There are "two separate statutory purses. In each, the ingathering and expending authority is different."

As we have seen, the Privy Council's *Silver Brothers* decision does not stand alone. It was merely a repetition of the point it had made in 1892 in the *Maritime Bank* case.[62]

---

62 "Their Lordships do not think it necessary to examine, in minute detail, the provisions of the Act of 1867, which nowhere profess to curtail in any respect the rights and privileges of the Crown, or to disturb the relations then subsisting between the Sovereign and the Provinces. The object of the Act was neither to weld the Provinces into one, nor to subordinate Provincial governments to a central authority, but to create a Federal government in which they should all be represented, entrusted with the exclusive administration of affairs in which they had a common interest, each province retaining its independence and autonomy. That

The Federal Parliament's constitutional authority to levy taxes (ingather money) and its power to expend that money is limited to "the due performance" of its "constitutional functions." Those functions do not include either raising money or spending it for the performance of any of the constitutional functions of a province. As section 102 of the *BNA Act* explicitly states, Parliament's authority to appropriate the public's money is limited to the "Public Service of Canada" and does not extend to the "Public Service" of any province.

It is therefore not surprising that when the Dominion appealed the Supreme Court's decision to the Privy Council, the Privy Council rejected all the arguments put to it by St. Laurent and his colleagues and rejected the dissenting "reasons" given by Chief Justice Duff.

It is not surprising because, in the first place, the Privy Council had held, in 1881, that control of "insurance" fell within section 92(13), "property and civil rights in the Province," and was therefore a matter within the exclusive competence of the provincial legislature(s).[63] Secondly, the *Employment and Social Insurance Act* did not "purport to deal with any special emergency" and accordingly was not supported by Parliament's "Peace Order and Good Government" power. That left to be disposed of, only, Duff's interpretation (or misinterpretation) of section 102 and the "public property" argument. The Privy Council's judgment on these points was delivered by Lord Atkin in this language:[64]

> "It only remains to deal with the argument which found favour with the Chief Justice and Davis, J. that the legislation can be supported under the enumerated heads, 1 and 3 of s. 91 of the British North America Act, 1867: (1) The public debt and property,

object was accomplished by distributing, between the Dominion and the Provinces, all power executive and legislative, and all public property and revenues which had previously belonged to the Provinces; so that the Dominion Government should be vested with such of these powers, property, and revenues as were necessary for the due performance of its constitutional functions, and that the remainder should be retained by the Provinces for the purposes of Provincial government. *But, in so far as regards those matters which by sect. 92 are specially reserved for provincial legislation, the legislation of each province continues to be free from the control of the Dominion, and as supreme as it was before the passing of the Act.*"

63 *Citizens Insurance Company* v. *Parsons* (1881) 7 App. Cas. 96.
64 *A.G. Canada* v. *A.G. Ontario*, [1937] A.C. 355 at 366-367.

namely (3) The raising of money by any mode or system of taxation. Shortly stated, the argument is that the obligation imposed upon employers and persons employed is a mode of taxation: that the money so raised becomes public property, and that the Dominion have then complete legislative authority to direct that the money so raised, together with assistance from money raised by general taxation, shall be applied in forming an insurance fund and generally in accordance with the provisions of the Act.

That the Dominion may impose taxation for the purpose of creating a fund for special purposes and may apply that fund for making contributions in the public interest to individuals, corporations or public authorities, could not as a general proposition be denied. Whether in such an Act as the present compulsion applied to an employed person to make a contribution to an insurance fund out of which he will receive benefit for a period proportionate to the number of his contribution is in fact taxation it is not necessary finally to decide. It might seem difficult to discern how it differs from a form of compulsory insurance, or what the difference is between a statutory obligation to pay insurance premiums to the State or to an insurance company. But assuming that the Dominion has collected by means of taxation a fund, it by no means follows that any legislation which disposes of it is necessarily within Dominion competence.

It may still be legislation affecting the classes of subjects enumerated in s. 92 and, if so, would be ultra vires. In other words, Dominion legislation even though it deals with Dominion property, may yet be so framed as to invade civil rights within the Province, or encroach upon the classes of subjects which are reserved to Provincial competence. It is not necessary that it should be a colourable device, or a pretense. If on the true view of the legislation it is found that in reality in pith and substance the legislation invades civil rights within the Province, or in respect of other classes of subjects otherwise encroaches upon the provincial field, the legislation will be invalid. To hold otherwise would afford the Dominion an easy passage into the Provincial domain. In the present case, their Lordships agree with the majority of the Supreme Court in holding that in pith and substance this Act is an insurance Act affecting the civil rights of employers and employed in each Province, and as such is invalid."

The Privy Council made the same point in respect to "spending" as it had made in respect of taxation in the *Insurance Act* case. Neither the federal power to tax nor the federal power to spend is unlimited. Both require that the tax or spending (appropriation) legislation in question must be a law made "in relation to" a subject matter otherwise within Parliament's jurisdiction, i.e. one or more of the subject matters enumerated in section 91. Neither taxation nor spending are themselves "division of powers" classifications. The judgments of the Supreme Court and of the Privy Council in the *Unemployment Insurance* case is not only consistent with *Silver Brothers* but reinforces the validity of the principles it declared. It should also be noted that the same Privy Council speaking through Lord Atkin delivered another judgment on the same day (January 28, 1937) striking down another federal statute enacted by the Bennet government as part of his Canadian "New Deal Program." It was in that case that Lord Atkin described federal and provincial legislative powers as separated inside "watertight compartments."[65]

If the separate "statutory purses" are confined in separate watertight compartments (as they are), then there cannot possibly be unlimited federal powers to tax or to spend.

If it were otherwise as both the Supreme Court and the Privy Council noted, then the Federal Parliament could assume jurisdiction to take over all of the legislative subject matters assigned by the *BNA Act* to the Provinces, by simply characterizing its laws as laws made "in relation to" taxation or spending. That of course is exactly what the Federal government has done by establishing a Crown Corporation to engage in the mortgage Insurance business (CMHC) and bribing the Provinces, through the offer of subsidies, to establish provincial health care regimes according to federally determined specifications which is what *The Canada Health Act* does.

I should mention here that those who say F.P.F.T. are lawful, pay little if any attention to the operative parts of Lord Atkin's judgment in the

---

65 A.G. Canada v. A.G. Ontario, [1937] A.C. 326.

Unemployment Insurance case. Some of them seize upon one sentence which is taken from it entirely out of context.

The sentence (taken out of context) reads:

> "That the Dominion may impose taxation for the purpose of creating a fund for special purposes and may apply that fund for making contributions in the public interest to individuals, corporations or public authorities could not, as a general proposition be denied."

However, that sentence was followed immediately by this statement:

> "If on the true view of (legislation such as the Employment and Social Insurance Act) it is found that in reality in pith and substance the legislation invades civil rights in the province or in respect of other classes of subjects otherwise encroaches upon the provincial field the legislation will be invalid."

As the *Employment and Social Insurance Act* purported to use federal money for provincial (Insurance) purposes, it was held by both the Supreme Court of Canada and the Privy Council to be invalid.

As I have pointed out before, there is no place in section 126 of the *BNA Act* for either the receipt or the expenditure by a province of any money whatsoever raised by federal taxation.

In addition, every cent that the Federal government receives as a result of federal taxation must be spent and spent *only* for the "*Public Service of Canada*" This is entirely consistent with the conclusion that F.P.F.T. are constitutionally prohibited and entirely inconsistent with any other rational conclusion.

Faced with Lord Atkin's rebuke in the *UEI* case, the Federal government asked the Parliament of Great Britain to amend the *BNA Act* to add "Unemployment Insurance" to the list of subject matters assigned to Parliament's jurisdiction. That amendment was made in 1940. It became section 91(2A). The Constitution was amended again in 1951 to add "Old Age Pensions" to the list of federal powers. That was done by section 94A. These amendments expanded federal power and at the same time diminished the powers which had originally been conferred by the *BNA Act* on the Provinces.

The seeking and the making of these amendments are, together with the amendment to section 118 made in 1907, consistent with the same conclusion. And in addition, the conclusion that F.P.F.T. are not authorized by the Constitution is consistent with the decision made on October 21, 1864 by the Fathers of Confederation of Quebec.

Government sponsored unemployment and pension schemes are examples of what are now called "social programs." The 1940 and 1951 amendments to the *BNA Act* did not transfer jurisdiction from the Provinces to Parliament over any other "social program", other than unemployment insurance and Old Age Pensions.

Nevertheless St. Laurent, when he became Prime Minister, calculated that he could get away with what he knew was a clear abuse of Parliament's constitutional authority, as provincial politicians had a long history of accepting (not complaining) about federal subsidies (bribes) to their governments.

According to an article authored in 1957 by the then Law Professor Pierre Elliot Trudeau, questioning the constitutionality of federal grants to Universities,[66] St Laurent had this to say about F.P.F.T. in a speech on November 12, 1956:

> "The Federal government has the absolute right to use indirect taxation for any purpose, and the right to impose direct taxation provided that it is destined to increase Canada's Consolidated Revenue Fund. With the approval of Parliament, it can then use this money to make gifts or grants-in-aid to individuals, institutions, Provincial governments, or even foreign governments. This is a royal prerogative which our constitution does not limit in any way."

This is truly an appalling statement for any Prime Minister of Canada to make, let alone by a prominent lawyer who was Canada's counsel in the *Insurance Act* and *Unemployment Insurance* cases. It is equally appalling to learn that St. Laurent got this idea from an article published in 1955 in the McGill University Law Journal[67] by a then prominent law professor, Professor F.A. Scott.[68]

---

66 *CitéLibre* February 1957.
67 The Constitutional Background of Taxation Agreements (1955), 2 McGill L. J. 1.
68 It is not without significance that F. R. Scott was a founder of the "league for Social

This is, in part, what Scott wrote:

> *"All public monies that fall into the Consolidated Revenue Funds of the federal and Provincial governments belong to the Crown. The Crown is a person capable of making gifts or contracts like any other person, to whomsoever it chooses to benefit. The recipient may be another government, or private individuals. The only constitutional requirement for Crown gifts is that they must have the approval of Parliament or legislature. This being obtained the Prince may distribute his largesse at will. Such gifts, of course, do not need to be accepted; the donee is always as free to reject as the donor to offer. Moreover, the Crown may attach conditions to the gift, failure to observe which will cause its discontinuance. These simple but significant powers exist in our constitutional law though no mention of them can be found in the BNA Act's. They derive from doctrines of the Royal Prerogative and the common law. They operate equally for the Crown in right of provinces as well as for the Crown in right of the Dominion. It would be as lawful for provinces to subsidize Ottawa as for Ottawa to subsidize provinces the only difference is that Ottawa is obliged by the constitution to pay certain statutory sums."* (Obviously a reference to s. 118).
>
> *The true answer is that none of these gifts is an invasion of anybody's rights in so far as constitutional law is concerned. Generosity in Canada is not unconstitutional. If the grants are undesirable, it must be for non-legal reasons."*

This statement is not only wrong it displays an abysmal ignorance of the origin and nature of "the Royal Prerogative" on the part of an eminent law professor, not to mention ignorance of the history of the *BNA Act* and the judgements of the Privy Council.

The Crown, which means the English Monarch, has never been "a person capable of making gifts or contracts like any other person" when acting in his or her official capacity; Queen Elizabeth II and all of her predecessors have *two* capacities, a *personal* and an *official* capacity.

---

reconstruction" (LSR) whose purpose was "to advocate socialist solutions in a Canadian context," a founding member of the C.C.F. and (in 1942) its National Chairman.

The Queen may, in her personal capacity, go shopping at Harrod's and contract to buy a hat, although I doubt that she has ever done so. She most certainly does not rule in her personal capacity. In their personal capacities, monarchs are subject to all of the vicissitudes of human beings such as illness, injury and eventually death. That is not the case with the Monarch's official capacity. In her official capacity, the Queen is not a human being but a "corporation sole."

In his lectures on the laws of England, read by Sir William Blackstone at the University of Oxford beginning in 1753, now to be found in the four volumes of Blackstone's Commentaries on the Laws of England, the author discussed the legal nature of "artificial persons, bodies politic, bodies corporate or corporations."[69]

Blackstone divided corporations into two classes, "aggregate" and "sole":

> *"Corporations aggregate consist of many persons united together into one society, and are kept up by a perpetual succession of members, so as to continue forever.*
>
> *Corporations sole consist of one person only and his successors, in some particular station, who are incorporated by law, in order to give them legal capacities and advantages, particularly that of perpetuity, which in their natural persons they could not have had. In this sense, the King is a sole corporation: so is a bishop ... and so is every parson and vicar.*
>
> *And so, while the property of a church may be vested in the parson, the property does not descend to the parson's heirs or be liable for his debts as it would if "it vested in his natural capacity.*
>
> *The law therefore has wisely ordained that the person (qua person) shall never die, any more than the king.*
>
> *By which means all the original rights of the parsonage are preserved entire to the successor: for the present incumbent and his predecessor who lived seven centuries ago, are in law one and the same person ....*

---

69 1 B.L. C. 8 p. 455.

> *The King ... is made a corporation to prevent ... the possibility of an interregnum or vacancy of the throne and to preserve the possessions of the Crown Entire."*[70]

Blackstone said that "the honour of originally inventing these" corporations belonged to the Romans, but corporations sole was invented by the "usual genius of the English Nation," "of which the Roman lawyers had no notion." In any event, the Queen is a corporation sole by reason of the common law.

This is why the English Crown Jewels, being the property of the State, are kept at the Tower of London rather than in the Queen's bedroom at Buckingham Palace.

It must then be obvious that the Monarch's Royal prerogative powers exists for the purposes of government and are exercised by the Monarch in his or her *official* capacity as a corporation sole.

When English Monarchs ruled (or thought they ruled) by the "divine right of kings" their powers were absolute. That idea did not survive King John's meeting with the Barons at Runnymede in 1215 and his signature on the *Magna Carta*.

C.L.O.C., quoting Professor Dicey" explains the Royal prerogative powers as: *"the residue of discretionary or arbitrary authority, which at any given time is left in the hands of the Crown."* As C.L.O.C. states: *"the prerogative is a branch of the common law because it is the decisions of the courts which have determined its existence and extent"* citing the *Case of Proclamations* (1611) 12, Co. rep. 74 holding that "the King hath no prerogative but that which the law of the land allows him."

On December 16, 1689 the English parliament enacted a statute entitled "An Act declaring the rights and liberties of the subject and setting the succession of the Crown." This enactment was a re-statement in statutory form of the Declaration of Rights presented by parliament to William and Mary in February 1689, inviting them to become joint sovereigns of England bringing an end to the "Glorious Revolution" against King James II. That statute is now variously referred to as the Bill of Rights 1688 or the Bill of Rights 1689. Its most significant provisions

---

[70] 1 B. Com. C. 18 pp. 455-458 — Hence the reason for the cry "The King is dead, Long Live the King."

prohibit the English Monarch from making or suspending any laws (including the imposition of taxes) without the authority of parliament so that Parliament became and remains the sovereign power in England.

C.L.O.C. acknowledges that this is so and that the English courts "established that only Parliament could authorize the expenditure of public funds."[71] As Halsbury's Laws of England explain[72] that the executive branch of English governments while nominally referred to as "the Crown," that word is used as a convenient symbol for the state. In practice, the Monarch's functions are now restricted principally to attaching her signature to various documents, the general policy of which have been previously determined by Ministers.[73]

In Canada, which is a federal state, the Crown is divided into the Crown in right of Canada (the Federal government) and the Crown in right of a Province (a Provincial government). However, the Monarch's role (and the role of her representatives in Canada, the Governor General and the Lieutenant Governors of the Provinces have been reduced "principally to attaching her signature to various Executive documents the nature and general policy of which have been previously determined by Ministers either individually or collectively." In practice then in England, the Queen signs whatever documents the Cabinet asks her to sign. In Canada the Governor-General does the same on her behalf.

Returning to Professor Scott's assertion that "the Prince may distribute his largesse at will," its corollary is that the Prince has no right to distribute any money or property that does not belong to him personally. A King, Queen, Prince or Princess has no right whatsoever to distribute any money belonging to the State without the State's authority. The Prince may be as generous as he likes in distributing his own money, but he is prohibited by the Constitution from taking any money out of the Consolidated Revenue Fund of Canada without Parliament's authorization. If the giving away of other people's money is "generosity," it is most certainly an invasion of their rights and clearly

---

71 C.L.O.C. section 1.9; for the proposition that only Parliament can authorize government spending C.L.O.C. cites the authority of the *Auckland Harbour* case — *Auckland Harbour Board v. The King* [1924] A. C. 318.
72 12(1) Hals. 4th, para. 3.
73 8(2) Hals. 4th, para. 351.

prohibited by the Constitution. The money deposited in a government's Consolidated Revenue Fund is taxpayer's money. It wasn't put there by "Pixies," and its expenditure is limited by sections 102 and 126 of the *BNA Act*. It is very difficult to believe that any law professor professing to opine upon Canadian Constitutional law could be entirely ignorant of those sections.

Since King John's encounter with the Barons at Runnymede, the English Monarch's Royal prerogative authority was gradually but inexorably diminished to the point that Queen Elizabeth II's role in the government whether in Britain or Canada is now merely ceremonial.

The only question concerning the Royal Prerogative, which is peculiar to Canada, is how those powers were divided by the *BNA Act* between the federal and provincial legislatures. That question was decided by the Privy Council in 1892 in the *Maritime Bank* case, which I have already referred to. However, as it is apparent that neither Professor Scott nor Louis St. Laurent had ever read it, I will quote the relevant passage from the judgment of the Privy Council again.

The facts were that the *Maritime Bank* went into liquidation and the government of New Brunswick claimed the right to be paid first, before the Bank's other creditors, as the debt was owing to the Crown in right of the Province of New Brunswick asserting the Royal prerogative of the Crown in right of New Brunswick.

One of the "special privileges" enjoyed by the Crown as part of "that pre-eminence the Sovereign enjoys over and above all other persons" pursuant to the Royal prerogative is to have debts to the Crown paid in preference to the debts of other creditors.

In the *Maritime Bank* case, counsel for the ordinary creditors sought to convince the court that the *BNA Act* had conferred *all Royal Prerogative powers on the federal crown (government) and that no provincial Crown government could claim any prerogative powers whatsoever including a preference for Crown debts.*

The Privy Council decided that the BNA Act had divided all governmental powers, including those based on the Royal Prerogative between the Federal and Provincial governments and accordingly, New Brunswick was entitled to assert the same Crown preference in the liquidation of the Maritime Bank as the federal Crown.

It is worth repeating here, Lord Watson's words:

> "Their Lordships do not think it necessary to examine, in minute detail, the provisions of the Act of 1867, which nowhere profess to curtail in any respect the rights and privileges of the Crown, or to disturb the relations then subsisting between the Sovereign and the provinces. The object of the Act was neither to weld the provinces into one, nor to subordinate Provincial governments to a central authority, but to create a Federal government in which they should all be represented, entrusted with the exclusive administration of affairs in which they had a common interest, each province retaining its independence and autonomy. That object was accomplished by distributing, between the Dominion and the provinces, all power executive and legislative, and all public property and revenues which had previously belonged to the provinces; so that the Dominion Government should be vested with such of these powers, property, and revenues as were necessary for the due performance of its constitutional functions, and that the remainder should be retained by the provinces for the purposes of Provincial government."

That judgment was delivered in 1892 and cited and relied upon by Canadian courts in many cases thereafter.[74] Yet it seems that a prominent law professor (Scott) and a prominent lawyer (St. Laurent) were not aware of what must be the most basic of all of the principles of the *BNA Act*.

It is also evident that neither Scott nor St. Laurent had even a nodding acquaintance with the deliberations and decisions of the Fathers of Confederation at Quebec in October 1864 concerning federal subsidies or grants in aid of the Provinces.

What the history of F.P.F.T. does show is the inclination to "interpret" the *BNA Act* in a way that promotes political expediency (St. Laurent) and political ideology (Scott). Those themes will be examined in the next chapter.

---

74 In *Bonanza Creek Gold Mining Company* v. *The King*, [1915] 1 A.C. 566 at 579 the Privy Council held that the *BNA Act* had divided governmental executive power including all Royal prerogative powers between Ottawa and the Provinces on the same basis that legislative power was divided.

CHAPTER 4

The **Proponent's** Propositions

The "Proponents" are those who have published arguments intended to support the conclusion that the Constitution authorizes Parliament to use its taxpayer's money to fund F.P.F.T., as Sir John A. Macdonald had proposed in 1864 that it should. The most prominent of these is today Dr. Peter Hogg, the author of C.L.O.C..[75]

In part 1 of this chapter, I will discuss the arguments that have been advanced in the past by the proponents generally as articulated by Professors F.R. Scott and G.V. Laforest. In part II, I will set out C.L.O.C's propositions.

PART I
The **Proponents'** Arguments

The most striking point I can make concerning the proponent's arguments is this: None of the proponents' writings even mention the Quebec Conference let alone the decisions made there by the Fathers of Confederation.

Professor Frank R. Scott was a member of the faculty of law at McGill

---

75 Dr. Peter Hogg formerly the Dean of the Osgoode Hall Law School, York University.

University, and its Dean from 1961 to 1964. He was, as well, a founder of the C.C.F., the Co-operative Commonwealth Federation, the predecessor of the N.D.P..

According to *Wikipedia*, Scott was greatly disturbed by the depression of the 1930's and as a result:

> "He, and the historian Frank Underhill, founded the League for Social Re-Construction to Advocate Socialist Solutions in a Canadian context."

It is clear from Scott's own words that his opinions concerning the constitutionality of F.P.F.T. were much more influenced by his political views rather than a dispassionate reading of the *BNA Act*. For example, the following is taken from Scott's article entitled "The Constitutional Background of Taxation Agreements"[76] published in 1955, which I referred to in Chapter 3.

"The Spending Power of Governments

> *All public monies that fall into the Consolidated Revenue Funds of the federal and Provincial governments belong to the Crown. The Crown is a person capable of making gifts or contracts like any other person, to whomsoever it chooses to benefit. The recipient may be another government, or private individuals. The only constitutional requirement for Crown gifts is that they must have the approval of Parliament or legislature. This being obtained the Prince may distribute his largesse at will. Such gifts, of course, do not need to be accepted; the donee is always as free to reject as the donor to offer. Moreover, the Crown may attach conditions to the gift, failure to observe which will cause its discontinuance. These simple but significant powers exist in our constitutional law though no mention of them can be found in the BNA Act's. They derive from doctrines of The Royal Prerogative and the common law. They operate equally for the Crown in right of provinces as well as for the Crown in right of the Dominion. It would be as lawful for provinces to subsidize Ottawa as for Ottawa to subsidize provinces: the only difference is that Ottawa is obliged by the constitution to pay certain statutory sums.*

---

76 (1995) 2 McGill L.J. 1.

> *These rules explain several interesting practices inherent in Canadian federalism. They explain why no amendment was necessary to the BNA Act in 1869 when the amount guaranteed to Nova Scotia was increased, if the federal Crown is obliged to give x dollars to a province, it does not violate its promise by giving x plus y dollars. It may excite the cupidity of other provinces by so doing, but that is not a legal matter."*

Contrary to this assertion, the interpretation of a statute is and always has been a *"legal matter."* It is a "legal matter" to opine, as Scott did, that a statute which authorizes Parliament to pay x dollars can be read as if it authorized Parliament to transfer to the Provinces any amount it chooses, so long as it is not less than x dollars. This is nonsense. As noted in the Introduction and to quote the Privy Council: "If the text (of the *BNA Act*) is explicit the text is conclusive, alike in what it directs and what it forbids,"[77] and it forbids any F.P.F.T. other than those provided for in section 118.

These words were spoken by the then Lord Chancellor (Earl Loreburn) on behalf of the Privy Council in holding that the Supreme Court of Canada was entitled, if asked by parliament, to advise upon the constitutionality of specific federal or provincial legislation to do so. There is no logical nor legal reason to suppose that if the *BNA Act* authorized (or required) the Federal government to transfer $100.00 of its taxpayer's money to the province of Ontario., it somehow had the authority to transfer $1,000.00 or $100,000.00 or any amount other than $100,000.00.

To say, as Scott did that "it would be as lawful for Provinces to subsidize Ottawa as for Ottawa to subsidize Provinces, displays Scott's ignorance of even the dictionary definition of "federalism." The essence of federalism is the independence of the Provincial governments from the government in Ottawa, and once again Scott makes clear that he has no knowledge whatsoever of Sir John A. Macdonald's motion made and defeated at the Quebec Conference.

In Scott's essay entitled "Our Changing Constitution,"[78] Scott described the Privy Council's judgment in the *Unemployment Insurance*

---

77 *A.G. Canada*, [1912] A.C. 571 at 583.
78 Essays on the Constitution; University of Toronto Press (1977).

case as "a judicial massacre" even though that judgment was simply the repetition, in other words, of the effect of section 102 of the *BNA Act*.

Before opining that F.P.F.T. were constitutional, it would have been appropriate, indeed necessary, for Professor Scott to have become acquainted with the proceedings of the Quebec Conference of 1864 which renders that opinion absurd.

Professor Browne's book (at page 77) contains the text of Macdonald's motion made on "Friday 21st October 1864" which included in the list of 32 matters respecting which Parliament was to be empowered to make laws, as item 30, "subsidies or grants in aid of the local (provincial) governments." Had he looked, Scott would also have found at pages 78 and 79 the list of federal powers the Fathers adopted, a list which did not include item 30, "subsidies or grants in aid of the local governments." The difference between the two lists is shown (at p. 78) to have been the result of …" the "adoption by the Honorable Mr. John A. Macdonald of certain amendments to his motion."

Macdonald's original list of federal powers contained 32 items but was not adopted. The list the Fathers decided to adopt contained only 28 and did not contain "subsidies or grants in aid of the Local Governments" (or any other language which included F.P.F.T.). It is obvious that Professor Scott was entirely ignorant of this crucial aspect of the history of our Constitution.

While section 118 provides for the Federal government's obligation to pay fixed amounts to the Provinces (and the corresponding right to fund those payments through taxation), it does not confer any additional rights or obligations. The Federal government's obligations under section 118 are to pay stipulated amounts so that its corresponding right to fund the discharge of those obligations through the imposition of taxes, is similarly limited.

Unlike laws that are made by legislatures to control the actions of *citizens*, Constitutions exist to control the action of *governments*. The purpose of the *BNA Act* was and is to confer law-making powers on the federal and provincial parliaments but the powers so conferred were necessarily limited. While the power to spend is conferred on both the Federal and Provincial governments, it is, in each case, limited by the provisions of sections 102 and 126. By those sections, the federal spending power is limited to the "*Public Service of Canada,*" and the spending power of each province is limited to the "Public Service of the Province." It is obvious that those spending powers are mutually exclusive as they were intended to be. Sections 102 and 126 are set forth in this chapter and should be read carefully. It seems that they have not been read carefully or otherwise by the proponents.

In the absence of an explicit federal power to make F.P.F.T., (a power Sir John A. Macdonald sought unsuccessfully to have included) the Federal government is prohibited by the Constitution from imposing taxes on federal tax payers to fund any payments to any province in excess of the payments it is required to make by section 118 of the *BNA Act*. All that is necessary for one to understand that F.P.F.T. (other than those originally required by section 118 and since 1907 [by the *British North America Act*, 1907] are illegal) is to read sections 102 and 126. Yet Scott does not mention either of those sections or offer any explanation as to how his opinions can be reconciled with their provisions. Nowhere in Scott's extensive writings on Canadian Constitutional law does he mention the proceedings of the Quebec Conference, Macdonald's motion, or how the Fathers of Confederation disposed of it. Yet, he said in *Our Changing* Constitution that as a student at the McGill Law School he was taught:

> "*To see the problems which (the BNA Act) was intended to remedy, to look at the conditions in the British North American Colonies in the 1860's and to seek the intentions of the Fathers of Confederation ... in all of the material available to historians.*"

It is obvious that Scott failed to take his own advice.

If he had, he would have discovered that a reliable source of "the intentions of the Fathers of Confederation" is to be found in the records assembled by Sir Joseph Pope, published in 1895 and (and now contained in Professor Browne's book). If Professor Browne could find them then Professor Scott could have, and should have found them, and more importantly avoided writing articles expressing opinions which the history of the *BNA Act* clearly contradicts.

Professor Browne's book (at page 77) contains the text of Macdonald's motion made on "Friday 21st October 1864" which included in the list of 32 matters respecting which Parliament was to be empowered to make laws including (as item 30) "subsidies or grants in aid of the local (Provincial) governments."

Macdonald's original list of federal powers contained 32 items. The list the Fathers adopted contained only 28 and did not contain:

> "*subsidies or grants in aid of the Local Governments*" *or any other language which included F.P.F.T..*

In other words, "them that made" the *BNA Act* deliberately and specifically decided that the federal parliament *would not be authorized to make F.P.F.T.*. There cannot be any doubt as to the accuracy of that conclusion, and the *BNA Act* must be interpreted accordingly.

I will turn now to another proponent, Professor G. V. LaForest, the author of a book entitled, "*The Allocation of the Taxing Power Under the Canadian Constitution.*"[79]

In Chapter 2 of this book, which is titled "*The Federal Power of Taxation*", La Forest makes reference to the broad taxing powers of the U.S. Federal government, noting that it "contrasts sharply with the Canadian position" as articulated by the Privy Council in the *Insurance Act* case. With respect to F.P.F.T., La Forest said that their legitimacy have been variously justified as flowing from the (Royal) prerogative, (citing F.R. Scott), the P.O.G.G. power in the opening words of section 91, and section 91(1A) "The public debt and property)." It is clear that, "Public Debt and Property as used in section 91 of the *BNA Act* means *federal debt and property* — as C.L.O.C. states in section 29.2. While he made reference to section 102 of the *BNA Act*, his comments on their meaning and significance can only be described as bizarre. This is what he said:

> "*It could be argued that section 102 of the British North America Act establishing a Consolidated Revenue Fund "to be appropriated for the Public Service of Canada" limits the spending and lending powers to purposes falling within the federal legislative sphere if one reads the phrase as referring to federal objects. But if one reads the section along with the federal legislative power*

---

79 Originally published by the Canadian Tax Foundation in 1969, Second Edition published in 1981.

> over public property, that objection cannot be maintained. "Public property," ... has been construed to comprise every kind of asset and the power to regulate it is given "notwithstanding anything in this Act." Consequently Parliament's discretion under section 91(1A) of determining what objects are and which are not within the scope of the words "for the Public Service of Canada" is not more restricted than it is under any other head of power.; i.e., the legislation is valid as long as it does not amount to a regulatory scheme falling within provincial powers."

Look again at section 102 and read it in the context of section 126:

> "**102.** All Duties and Revenues over which the respective Legislature of Canada, Nova Scotia, and New Brunswick before and at the Union had and have Power of Appropriation, except such Portions thereof as are by this Act reserved to the respective legislatures of the provinces, or are raised by them in accordance with the special Powers conferred on them by this Act, shall form One Consolidated Revenue Fund, to be appropriated for the Public Service of Canada in the Manner and subject to the Charges in this Act provided."

> "**126.** Such Portions of the Duties and Revenues over which the respective Legislatures of Canada, Nova Scotia, and New Brunswick had before the Union Power of Appropriation as are by this Act reserved to the respective Governments or Legislatures of the provinces, and all Duties and Revenues raised by them in accordance with the special Powers conferred upon them by this Act, shall in ach Province form One Consolidated Revenue Fund to be appropriated for the Public Service of the Province."

When read in context, it is clear that sections 102 and 126 makes a vital distinction between federal spending on the one hand and provincial spending on the other. The Public Service of Canada cannot be the Public Service of any Province.

The author of this language ("them that made it") was the Parliament of the United Kingdom sitting at Westminster, but when Scott speaks of "Parliament's discretion" under the *BNA Act* he is referring to the Canadian Parliament sitting in Ottawa which was not given any discretion whatsoever to interpret the *BNA Act*. There is only one branch of

Canadian government which possesses the right to interpret any of the provisions of the *BNA Act* and thus to determine the meaning of the words "Public Service of Canada," and that is the judiciary which is obliged to interpret any and all of the legislation it is called upon to interpret according to the intent of "them that made it" and in no other manner. What matters is the words the legislature has used, and the "golden rule" has always been that "the words of a statute must be taken in the ordinary, natural, grammatical sense which they bore the day after the statute was passed."[80]

To say (as Scott did) that Parliament has a "discretion" to interpret the language of the *BNA Act* displays an abysmal ignorance of the law in general and the history of the *BNA Act* in particular.

As is painfully obvious, the "Public Service of Canada" is used in section 102 in contradistinction to "The Public Service of the Province" in section 126 (which La Forest neglected to mention). When read in context the Public Service of Canada means appropriations for purposes falling within the federal legislative sphere. The "Public Service of Canada" cannot have any other meaning, just as the "Public Service of the Province" can have no meaning other than purposes falling within the jurisdiction of the provincial legislatures.

Thus the "Public Debt and property" in section 91 (1A) means *federal* debt and property, not provincial debt or property.

While Parliament may legislate with respect to federal property, it has no jurisdiction whatsoever to decide whether or not any legislation whether federal or provincial is or is not constitutionally valid. That decision is reserved exclusively[81] to the courts. To say that Parliament has the constitutional right to decide in its *"discretion"* "what objects are, and which are not" within the scope of the words "for the Public Service of Canada" is preposterous. It is telling that La Forest cites as the authority for his preposterous proposition the *dissenting* judgment of Chief Justice Duff in the *Unemployment Insurance* case.

A dissenting opinion is, by definition, an opinion with which the majority of a multi-judge court disagreed, and accordingly stands for nothing in law, other than the conclusion that the law is the opposite

---

80 *Mattison v. Hart* (1854) ER 1498.
81 C.L.O.C. Section 29.2.

of what the dissenter asserted it to be. In the *Unemployment Insurance* case, the ultimate decision was not made by Duff. It was made by the Privy Council overruling Duff and explicitly rejecting Duff's opinion. It is of interest to note that in the arguments put to the Privy Council in that case by counsel for the Federal government (Louis St. Laurent), he did not even argue that Duff's opinions were meritorious. Rather St. Laurent argued that unemployment in Canada had become such a significant and wide-spread problem that only the Parliament of Canada was equipped to deal with it by using its P.O.G.G. power. There is no support whatever for La Forest's view to be found in the *U.I.* case.

While LaForest mentions the *Silver Brothers* case in his book, his reference to it belies the assumption that he had ever read it, or if he had, understood it. The case is cited in Chapter 1 ("Historical Introduction") and in Chapter 2 ("The Federal Power of Taxation") in both instances only to explain the Crown's prerogative right to claim preference for Crown debts over others' debts in cases of bankruptcy. It is not cited for any other purpose. Laforest did not indicate what the case was about or what the Privy Council decided.

In the official reports of the judgments of the Privy Council, the Editors provide a "Head Note" at the beginning which is then followed by a summary of the reasons for judgment as articulated by the Judges that decided it. What follows is the head note to the *Silver Brothers* case with the portion that is relevant to the legality of F.P.F.T. presented in bold type:

> **"ON APPEAL FROM THE SUPREME COURT OF CANADA**
>
> *Canada — Interpretation of statute — Crown — Crown debts — Priority — Competing Dominion tax and Provincial tax — Legislative power — Bankruptcy — Taxation — British North America Act, 1878 (30 and 31 Vict. c/ S.), s. 91, heads 3, 21 — Interpretation Act (R.S. Con., 1907, c. 1) s. 16*
>
> *By s. 17 of the (Dominion) Special War Revenue Act, 1915, as amended in 1923 (but since repealed), liability to the Crown for the excise taxes thereby imposed was to rank for payment in priority to all other claims of whatsoever kind save administration expenses. By s. 1357 of the R.S. Queb. 1908, all sums due to the*

> Crown, in respect of Provincial taxes are to constitute a privileged debt ranking after law costs. By s. 16 of the Interpretation Act (R.S. Can., 1906, c. 1) no provision in any Act is to affect the Crown unless it is expressly stated therein that the Crown is to be bound thereby.
>
> In a bankruptcy in the Province of Quebec the assets were insufficient to discharge both a sum due for tax under the Dominion statue above mentioned and a sum due for Provincial taxes.
>
> Held, that it would have been competent to the Parliament of Canada under the British North America Act, 1867, s. 91, head 21 (bankruptcy), or head 3 (taxation), to enact the statute of 1915 so as to prejudice the rights of the Province, but that having regard to s. 16 of the Interpretation Act the statute had to be read as though it provided that the priority enacted should not operate so as to diminish any right of the Crown in any Province; the result was that the two debts would run pari passu as claimed by the Province.
>
> There is only one Crown, but by legislation assented to by the Crown revenue and property vested in the Dominion are distinguished from revenue and property vested in a Province. There are two separate and statutory purses; in each the ingathering and expending authority is different."

It matters not whether the division of legislative power between Ottawa and the Provinces is described as placed in watertight compartments or separate statutory purses, the point is that Parliament is bound by that division and has no discretion whatever to decide that the Public Service of Canada includes in whole or in part the Public Service of any province.

It is highly unlikely that any Canadian constitutional lawyer could possibly have been unaware of Lord Atkins judgment in the 1937 *Labour Conventions* case[82] describing Canada, in its position of independence, (achieved as a result of the 1931 statute of Westminster), as a "ship of state" which "now sails on larger ventures and into foreign waters

---

82 A.G. Canada v. A. G. Ontario, [1937] A.C. 306 at 354.

(but) still retains the *watertight compartments*" (separating federal from provincial powers), "*which are an essential part of her original structure.*"

In the *Silver Brothers* case, the Privy Council used another, but a similar metaphor, ("separate statutory purses") to describe the result of the division of powers provided for in the *BNA Act*, of which sections 102 and 126 are clearly examples.

In a paper published in *Canadian Bar Review* in 1989 entitled "*Federalism and the Myth of the Federal Spending Power*"[83] Professor Andrew Petter, of the Faculty of Law at the University of Victoria[84] said that he had found the lack of academic controversy among legal academics as to the constitutionality of F.P.F.T. "difficult to fathom."

Professor Petter described the common belief among the courts, constitutional scholars and most political actors before the Second World War as the belief "that a clear division of political responsibilities between two co-ordinate orders of government was an essential characteristic of the Canadian State." This he described as "co-ordinate federalism." The use of F.P.F.T. which began in earnest after World War II was described as "administrative federalism" which he described as a circumvention of the federal Parliament's legislative jurisdiction. He then asked this rhetorical question:

> "What accounts for the uncritical stance (concerning F.P.F.T.) adopted by these scholars? There are a number of probable explanations. For some, support for administrative federalism has stemmed from their desire to broaden the authority of the central government. It is no coincidence that one of the earliest and most outspoken proponents of the federal spending power was F.R. Scott, as ardent a centralist as this country is likely to see. For others, support of the spending power appears to be related to their support for political initiatives with which it has been associated. After all, what "progressive" constitutionalist[85] in the post-war period would want to be seen objecting to Federal government support of highways, education and universal health insurance?"

---

83 (1989) 69 CBR 34.
84 He is now the President of the University.
85 In this context "progressive" means a person who favours social reform i.e. changes. I will have more to say about "progressives" in Chapter 5.

Professor Petter had this to say concerning F.P.F.T. specifically:

> "*Underlying the federal position, and the position of many constitutional writers, is the belief that spending is somehow different from, and less in need of constitutional containment than, other forms of governmental activity. Scott and Driedger equate spending with gifting, and express shock at the suggestion that private persons could make gifts but that governments could not. Hogg states (in C.L.O.C.):*
>
>> '*There is a distinction, in my view, between compulsory regulation, which can obviously be accomplished only by legislation enacted within the limits of legislative power, and spending or lending or contracting, which either imposes no obligations on the recipient ... or obligations which are voluntarily assumed by the recipient ... There is no compelling reason to confine spending or lending or contracting within the limits of legislative power, because in those functions the government is not purporting to exercise any peculiarly governmental authority over its subjects.*'
>
> *With respect, the views of these scholars have a sense of unreality about them. What they seem to forget is that governmental spending is not an isolated activity. When a government spends, it must derive the revenue from somewhere. The way that government usually does this is through the imposition of taxation something which is, without doubt, the exercise of a "peculiarly governmental authority." The importance of the Privy Council judgment in the Employment and Social Insurance Act Reference is that it recognized this relationship and rejected arguments that it should characterize the spending function as though it were unrelated to the taxing function. Rather, it correctly saw them as part and parcel of a single redistributive activity.*"

Professor Petter recognized that there was no relevant difference between a federal *Appropriation Act* authorizing federal spending and any other federal legislation. The question is the same in every case, and it is, whether the law made by Parliament is made "in relation to" a federal subject matter or not. If it is, it is constitutionally valid. If not, it is *ultra vires*.

As Professor Petter put it:

> "There is no basis in language or in logic for suggesting that when Parliament authorizes expenditures of funds with respect to some matter it acts any less "in relation" to that matter than when it regulates with respect to the same matter."

As "spending" is not, as such, a head of federal power, the question will always be whether the spending which Parliament purports to authorize is itself authorized by a law made *in relation* to a subject matter, (other than "spending") which is within Parliament's legislative jurisdiction to enact. In other words, the question is whether the federal *Appropriation Act* which purports to authorize the spending is constitutionally valid federal legislation. In other words, whether the law in question can or cannot be characterized as "regulation" is utterly irrelevant. There is no distinction to be made for the purposes of constitutional law.

In Professor Petter's opinion, unconditional F.P.F.T. such as equalization payments are constitutional under the "National dimensions component" of the P.O.G.G. power. This is his argument:

> "Given that equalization of wealth among regions is a discrete function that falls beyond the scope of provincial legislative power, a federal law whose purpose is limited to equalization should be sustainable on the basis of the national dimensions component of the peace, order and good government power. Moreover, since 1982, the Constitution has explicitly acknowledged the right of the Federal governments to make "equalization payments to ensure that Provincial governments have sufficient revenues to provide reasonably comparable levels of public services at reasonably comparable levels of taxation": Constitution Act, 1982, s. 36(2)"[86]

I will discuss the so-called "national dimensions" doctrine shortly, but it is first necessary to point out that contrary to Petter's assertion, section 36 of the *Constitution Act* 1982 has not "explicitly acknowledged the right of the Federal government to make equalization payments."

As noted in the Introduction, section 36 of the *Constitution Act* begins by stating that its provisions *do not alter* the legislative authority of Parliament in any way. As the reader now knows, Parliament does

---

86 Footnote 60.

not have the legislative authority to make F.P.F.T. of any kind, other than those originally required by section 118 of the *BNA Act*. Consequently, section 36 of the *Constitution Act 1982* has declared itself irrelevant to the constitutionality or otherwise of F.P.F.T..

Section 36 *does not create the right of the Federal government to make "equalization payments." It mistakenly assumes it.*

Legislative mistakes which are sometimes described as "lapses" or "blunders" cannot be rectified by the courts composed of un-elected judges. They can only be corrected by the legislature that made the mistake.

As Lord Loreburn observed in *Bristol Guardians v. Bristol Waterworks Co.*:[87]

> "After all, it is not our (the Court's) function to repair blunders that are to be found in legislation. They must be corrected by the Legislature."

As section 36 is now "enshrined" in the Constitution it can be changed by an amendment to the Constitution *but only by an amendment*. As presently "enshrined" section 36 is for all legal purposes not only a blunder but a legal nullity. There is therefore no doubt that the law as stated in the *Bristol Waterworks* case is the law in Canada and the only way to change section 36 is by a formal amendment to it.

In *United Fisherman and Allied Workers Union v. B.C. Provincial Council*[88] the Chief Justice said, on behalf of the Supreme Court of Canada, that the failure of Parliament to amend the *Canada Labour Code's* (the legislation's) definition of the word "employer" to match the definition of "employee" was undoubtedly a lapse (i.e. a blunder) but *I do not see how a court can add words to (a) statute unless they are implicit.*[89]

It is abundantly clear that section 36 of the *Constitution Act 1982* does not and was not intended to amend any of the other provisions of the *BNA Act* and does not do so either explicitly or implicitly.

Lastly the proponents suggest (as Professor Petter did) that F.P.F.T. can be viewed as a legitimate exercise of Parliament's power to make

---

87 [1914] A.C. 379 at 388 (H. of L.)
88 [1978] 2 S.C.R. 97.
89 *The Shorter Oxford English Dictionary.*

laws for the peace order and good government of Canada, which appear in the opening words of section 91, which are as follows:

> "91. It shall be lawful for the Queen, by and with the Advice and Consent of the Senate and House of Commons, to make Laws for the Peace, Order, and good Government of Canada, in relation to all Matters not coming within the Classes of Subjects by this Act assigned exclusively to the Legislatures of the provinces; and for greater Certainty, but not so as to restrict the Generality of the foregoing Terms of this Section, it is hereby declared that (notwithstanding anything in this Act) the exclusive Legislative Authority of the Parliament of Canada extends to all Matters coming within the Classes of Subjects next hereinafter enumerated; that is to say ..."

C.L.O.C. devotes an entire chapter to the P.O.G.G. power and according to C.L.O.C., the federal P.O.G.G. power consists of three branches: the "Gap branch", the "National concern branch" and the "Emergency branch."

The gap branch is illustrated by the "radio" reference decision of the Privy Council of 1932.[90] Radio communication was unknown in 1867 and is therefore not specifically mentioned in the *BNA Act*. The Privy Council held that this "gap" in the Constitution might be filled up by assigning that subject to the federal P.O.G.G. power, but only in cases in which it could be said that the "gap" existed as a result of inadvertence. For example, it was argued in the *Parsons*[91] case in 1881 that the Dominion could not authorize the incorporation of companies with Dominion-wide objects as the power of the Provinces to incorporate companies was limited by section 92(11) to the incorporation of companies with "provincial objects." The Privy Council held that Parliament was authorized to incorporate companies with Dominion-wide objects by reason of "its general power over all matters not coming within the classes of subjects assigned exclusively to the legislatures of the Provinces," which did not include the incorporation of companies other than those "with provincial objects ...."

In contrast, the lack of Parliament's authority to make laws "in

---

90 Re: Regulation and Control of Radio Communication in Canada, A.C. 304.
91 *Citizens Insurance Co. v. Parsons*

relation to," "subsidies or grants in aid of the (Provinces)" was not inadvertent, it was intentional. It would be absurd for a court to reinsert into the *BNA Act* a power which the Fathers had deliberately decided Parliament should not have. Consequently, the "gap" branch of P.O.G.G. cannot possibly justify F.P.F.T..

The "emergency" branch of the P.O.G.G. power is (not surprisingly), limited to emergencies. The lack of an explicit power to make F.P.F.T. is not an emergency, it existed on July 1, 1867, and the "emergency" branch of the P.O.G.G. power has no application whatsoever.

Much the same observation can be made about "National concern" or as it is sometimes described the "National dimensions" aspect of P.O.G.G..

In the *Queen v. Hauser*[92] the Supreme Court upheld the validity of the federal *Narcotic Control Act* on the ground that the *Act* was intended to deal with "a genuinely new problem." The lack of federal power to authorize F.P.F.T. cannot possibly be described as "new" nor as a "problem." It is what the Fathers' intended.

As the Privy Council held in the *Maritime Bank* case, the *BNA Act* was intended to distribute:

> "between the Dominion and the provinces all powers executive and legislative, … so that the Dominion \ Government should be vested with such of these powers … as were necessary for the due performance of its Constitutional functions."

The making of F.P.F.T. has never been a federal constitutional function. In order to uphold the constitutional validity of F.P.F.T. it would have to be held, that F.P.F.T. is one of the Dominion's constitutional functions. That is impossible in the light of the failure of Sir John A. Macdonald's motion of October 21, 1864.

We have therefor come full circle. As the Supreme Court has held:

> "the Constitution must be interpreted with a view to discerning the structure of government it seeks to implement."[93]

That structure *excludes F.P.F.T. as it was intended to do.*

---

92 (1979), 1 S.C.R. 984.
93 Reference Re: *Senate Reform*, [2014] S.C.C. 22.

PART 2
The C.L.O.C.'s Arguments

C.L.O.C.'s arguments for the constitutionality of F.P.F.T. are set out in its section 6.8(a) which begins by acknowledging that:

> *"When the Federal government makes an unconditional grant to a province, the grant is of course used by the province for its own purposes. This means that funds raised by federal taxes end up being applied to objects which are outside federal legislative authority."*

As the imposition of federal taxes and the spending of the resulting revenue must be authorized by the Constitution, federal legislation purporting to authorize either for the purposes of F.P.F.T. is beyond the federal Parliament's jurisdiction, *ultra vires*, and a legal nullity. The only exceptions to this conclusion are the transfers originally required to be made by section 118.

Even C.L.O.C. recognizes that there is a problem with its assertion that F.P.F.T. are constitutional. This is apparent from this statement in section 6.8(a):

> *"What is the constitutional basis for federal grants to the provinces, and for federal involvement in shared-cost programmes that are outside federal legislative competence? The only possible basis is the "spending power" of the federal Parliament, a power which is nowhere explicit in the Constitution Act, 1867, but which must be inferred from the powers to levy taxes (s. 91(3)), to legislate in relation to "public property" (s. 91(1A)), and to appropriate federal funds (s. 106) [sic]. Plainly the Parliament must have the power to spend the money which its taxes yield, and to dispose of its own property. But of course, the issue is whether this spending power authorizes payments for objects which are outside federal legislative competence."*

The first sentence of this passage is a question to which C.L.O.C. states there is only one "possible" answer, but C.L.O.C.'s answer is based on the utterly false assertion that the "spending power of the federal parliament *(is) nowhere explicit in the Constitution Act 1867."*

This is an egregious error which entirely eviscerates C.L.O.C.'s argument. The spending power of the Federal government *is explicitly provided for in the sections to be found in Part VIII of the BNA Act and in particular by section 102*. Here are those sections:

"VIII. REVENUES; DEBTS; ASSETS; TAXATION"

"102. All Duties and Revenues over which the respective Legislatures of Canada, Nova Scotia, and New Brunswick before and at the Union had and have Power of Appropriation, except such Portions thereof as are by this Act reserved to the respective Legislatures of the provinces, or are raised by them in accordance with the special Powers conferred on them by this Act, shall form One Consolidated Revenue Fund, to be appropriated for the Public Service of Canada in the Manner and subject to the Charges in this Act provided."

"103. The Consolidated Revenue Fund of Canada shall be permanently charged with the Costs, Charges and Expenses incident to the Collection, Management, and Receipt thereof, and the same shall form the First Charge thereon, subject to be reviewed and audited in such Manner as shall be ordered by the Governor General in Council until the Parliament otherwise provides."

"104. The annual Interest of Public Debts of the several provinces of Canada, Nova Scotia, and New Brunswick at the Union shall form the Second Charge on the Consolidated Revenue Fund of Canada."

"105. Unless altered by the parliament of Canada, the Salary of the Governor General shall be Ten thousand Pounds Sterling Money of the United Kingdom of Great Britain and Ireland, payable out of the Consolidated Revenue Fund of Canada, and the same shall form the Third Charge thereon."

"106. Subject to the several Payments by this Act charged on the Consolidated Revenue Fund of Canada, the same shall be appropriated by the parliament of Canada for the Public Service, (meaning the Public Service of Canada.)"

As a result of the presence of these sections in the *BNA Act*, all federal revenues from whatever source, *must* be deposited in "One Consolidated Revenue Fund" and "appropriated," (which is to say spent) "for the "Public Service of Canada." The Public Service of Canada is used in contra-distinction to the Public Service of a province as is made clear by section 126:

> "**126.** *Such Portions of the Duties and Revenues over which the respective Legislatures of Canada, Nova Scotia, and New Brunswick had before the Union Power of Appropriation as are by this Act reserved to the respective Governments or Legislatures of the provinces, and all Duties and Revenues raised by them in accordance with the special Powers conferred upon them by this Act, shall in each province form One Consolidated Revenue Fund to be appropriated for the Public Service of the Province."*

There can be no doubt whatsoever that "The Public Service of Canada" does not include the public service of any province or that F.P.F.T. are not used for the Public Service of Canada and are therefore clearly and absolutely prohibited unless made in accordance with the 1904 amendment to section 118 of the *BNA Act* which authorizes F.P.F.T. and that gives rise to the rule which is so old it is expressed in Latin, i.e., *"Expressio unius est exclusion alterius"* — the expression of one thing is the exclusion of all others.

Accordingly, the only F.P.F.T. authorized by the *BNA Act* are those provided for in the 1904 amendment to S. 118.

> *"There can for reasons I cannot begin to understand, the author of C.L.O.C. has provided as an Appendix I to his book, a version of the BNA Act in which sections 102 to 105 and 126 have been deliberately omitted. There can be no explanation for this, and none is given."*

Under the *BNA Act*, (as enacted) the spending power of the federal Parliament is limited to the Public Service of Canada, which means, to purposes that are otherwise within its legislative competence, or in the words of the Privy Council (in the *Maritime Bank* case), *the powers* "necessary for the due performance of its constitutional functions."

The funding of F.P.F.T., is manifestly not and never has been necessary for the due performance of any of the Federal government's constitutional functions as the Fathers of Confederation decided on October 21, 1864. The author of C.L.O.C. is entirely ignorant of this crucial historical fact which C.L.O.C. makes clear in this statement, in its section 6.8 which states the following:

> "It is true that the framers of the Constitution could hardly have foreseen the rise of the welfare state with its enormous growth in provincial responsibilities. But to interpret the Constitution as impliedly forbidding the richer regions of the country from helping the poorer ones is to attribute a narrowness of visions to the framers which is thoroughly at odds with what we know of them. This is indeed the "watertight compartments view of federalism carried to an extreme."

Contrary to C.L.O.C.'s assertion, the Constitution does not "*impliedly*" forbid "the richer regions of the country from helping the poorer ones," it does so *explicitly, deliberately,* and *unambiguously* as the records of the Quebec Conference for October 21 1864 indisputably demonstrate and section 102 of the *BNA Act* confirms. Whether or not the Fathers' decision concerning F.P.F.T. engenders C.L.O.C.'s praise or contempt could not be more irrelevant.

Even if you could take the provisions of the *BNA Act* as evidence that the policy choices it implements were the policy choices of heartless right-wing zealots, no judge or court has the slightest jurisdiction to change those provisions. In *R: v. McIntosh* (1995).[94] The Supreme Court of Canada declared that the law applicable to statutory interpretation includes this proposition: "where, by the use of clear language capable of only one meaning anything is enacted by (a) legislature it must be enforced however harsh or absurd or contrary to common sense the result may be."

I do not concede that the Father's "policy" decision concerning F.P.F.T. can be criticized on moral or ideological grounds. It can't be. The point is that even if it could be, the *BNA Act* is to be interpreted as written and not as the author of C.L.O.C. would have liked it to have been written.

I should also note in passing that "watertight" is an absolute term. A

---

94 (1995) 1 SCR 686 at para. 34.

compartment cannot be a little "watertight." It is either watertight or it is not. The word "watertight cannot be carried to an extreme", as it said these days, "it is what it is."

There can be no doubt that the Fathers' decision to reject F.P.F.T. was a policy choice which the Fathers had the right to make and did make.

As the Privy Council said in the *Companies Reference* case:[95]

> "It cannot be too strongly put that with the wisdom or expediency or policy of an Act, lawfully passed, no court has a word to say."

This is what C.L.O.C. has to say on this point (in section 12.2(g) under the heading "Wisdom or policy of legislation":

> "The idea underlying parliamentary sovereignty is that in a democratic society important public policy choice should be made in the elected legislative assemblies, and not by non-elected judges. It is often said, for example, that the courts have no concern with "the wisdom or expediency or policy" of a statue."

C.L.O.C. makes another argument for the constitutionality of F.P.F.T., set out in section 6.8(a) which Professor Petter demolished. The argument as stated by C.L.O.C. is this:

> "There is, a distinction, in my view between compulsory regulation, which can be accomplished only by legislation enacted within the limits of legislative power, and spending or contracting, which either imposes no obligations on the recipient (as in the case of unconditional grants) or obligations which are voluntarily assumed by the recipient (as in the case of a conditional grant loan or commercial contract). There is no compelling reason to confine spending or lending or contracting within the limits of legislative power because in those functions the government is not purporting to exercise any peculiarly governmental authority over its subjects."

There may be a distinction to be made between "compulsory regulation" and government "spending" but for the purposes of statutory interpretation, it is entirely devoid of any legal significance. The authority vested in the Parliament of Canada by section 91 of the *BNA*

---

95 *A.G. Ontario v. A.G. Canada*, (1912) A.C. 571 at 583.

Act is the authority to "make laws ... *in relation* to all matters not coming within the classes of subjects by this Act assigned exclusively to the Legislatures of the Provinces ...." It is *not* the authority to make laws "*regulating*" those subjects. The only subject matter that "confines" Parliament's legislative authority to "regulation" is section 91(2) "the regulation of Trade and Commerce." Whether or not the provisions of section 102, which confines federal spending, to "the Public Services of Canada," can be said to be "regulation" is completely and utterly irrelevant. To say, as C.L.O.C. does, that "there is no compelling reason to *confine* spending or lending or contracting within the limits of legislative power because **in those functions the government is not purporting to exercise any peculiarly governmental authority over its subjects**" is absolute nonsense. How does the author of C.L.O.C. suppose that the Federal government acquires the money required to finance "spending" or "lending" or "contracting" if not by taxation, which has to be *the exercise of the most peculiarly governmental authority over its subjects* it is possible to imagine? Even C.L.O.C. itself acknowledges (in section 31.1(a)) that the taxing authority of the Federal parliament is *confined* to objects which are otherwise within (and not beyond) federal legislative competence. This is how C.L.O.C. puts it:

> "*Needless to say, both the federal and provincial taxing powers are subject to the ordinary principles of classification and colourability that apply to all legislative powers. The pith and substance of a law that imposes a charge or a levy may be held to be some matter other than taxation, for example, insurance, unemployment insurance, banking, export trade, labour standards or marketing. In such cases, the validity of the law turns on whether the enacting legislative body had legislative authority over the true matter of the law. The enacting body's taxing power is irrelevant.*"[96]

The *Insurance Act* case of 1932 involved (not surprisingly) the constitutionality of the *Insurance Act*, which was a federal statute purporting to require insurance companies licensed to do business by a province, to acquire in addition to its provincial licence a licence under the federal *Act*. The *Insurance Act* case also involved another federal statute which

---

96 In *re: The Insurance Act of Canada* (1932) A.C. 41.

purported to impose a federal tax on those companies. The Privy Council struck down both statutes as *ultra vires* Parliament. With respect to the latter, the Privy Council had this to say:

> *"Now as to the power of the Dominion Parliament to impose taxation there is no doubt. But if the tax as imposed is linked up with an object which is illegal the tax for that purpose must fall.*
>
> *Their Lordships cannot do better than quote and then paraphrase a portion of the words of Duff J. in the Reciprocal Insurer's case. (1) He says: "In accordance with the principle inherent in these decisions their Lordships think it is no longer open to dispute that the Parliament of Canada cannot, by purporting to create penal sanctions under s. 91, head 27, appropriate to itself exclusively a field of jurisdiction in which, apart from such a procedure it could exert no legal authority, and that if, when examined as a whole, legislation in form criminal is found, in aspects and for purposes exclusively within the Provincial sphere to deal with matters committed to the provinces, it cannot be upheld as valid." If instead of the words create penal sanctions under s. 91, head 27" you substitute the words "exercise taxation powers under s. 91, head 3," and for the word "criminal" substitute "taxing", the sentence expresses precisely their Lordships' views."*

In other words, the Parliament of Canada cannot by purporting to impose federal taxation in relation to a subject matter, which is not otherwise within Parliament's legislative jurisdiction, which F.P.F.T. are clearly not, acquire the money required to fund F.P.F.T. Spending on F.P.F.T. is manifestly spending for the Public Service of a province which Parliament is prohibited from doing.

The *Insurance* case was decided on February 9, 1932. On October 22, of that year the Privy Council decided the *Silver Brothers* case[97] holding that (in the words of the headnote):

> *"There is only one Crown, but by legislation assented to by the Crown revenue and property vested in the Dominion are distinguished from revenue and property vested in a Province. There*

---

97 In *Re Silver Brothers Limited* (1932) A.C. 514.

are two separate statutory purses; in each the ingathering and expending authority is different."

Let me repeat. It is impossible to imagine the exercise of a more "peculiarly governmental authority over its subjects than subjecting them to taxation.

Nowhere in the hundreds of pages of C.L.O.C. is there any reference to the headnote of the *Silver Brothers* case as set out in the official law reports which contain the following:

> "There is only one Crown, but by legislation assented to by the Crown revenue and property vested in the Dominion are distinguished from revenue and property vested in a Province. There are two separate statutory purses: in each the ingathering and expending authority is different."

Clearly parliament is forbidden from taking money out of the federal purse raised by taxation that can only be imposed for legitimate federal purposes only and give it to the Provinces which are then (by reason of section 126 of the *BNA Act* obliged to spend it for provincial, not federal purposes".

The words used by Lord Atkin in delivering the judgment of the Privy Council in the *Unemployment Insurance* case bear repeating:

> "No one can doubt that the distribution (of powers) ... is one of the most essential conditions probably the most essential condition in the inter-provincial compact to which the British North America Act gives effect.
>
> While the (Canadian) ship of state now sails on larger ventures and into foreign waters she still retains the water-tight compartments which are an essential part of her original structure."[98]

This judgment was entirely consistent with the Privy Council's much earlier decision in the *Maritime Bank* case delivered in 1892 by Lord Watson, and whether or not the author of C.L.O.C. likes or dislikes the watertight metaphor is irrelevant.

Lastly, C.L.O.C. relies upon the reasons for judgment of the Supreme

---

98 A.G. Canada v. A.G. Ontario, (937) A.C. 326 at 351-354.

Court of Canada, delivered in 1991, in *Re: Canada Assistance Plan*,[99] ("C.A.P.") a judgment which seems to have been based upon the acceptance by that court of C.L.O.C.'s untenable arguments.

The author of C.L.O.C. was one of several counsel who appeared in the *Canada Assistance Plan* case and argued for the constitutionality of the C.A.P. statute. The Supreme Court's reasons for judgment were written by the late Justice John Sopinka. Sopinka's reasons for judgment clearly cited some twenty irrelevant decided cases, including an Australian case, but did not ever mention the *Insurance Act* case, *Silver Brothers* or the *Unemployment Insurance* case. Nor did Sopinka mention the Quebec Conference and Sir John A. Macdonald's October 1864 motion or its rejection.

The C.A.P. purported to authorize the government of Canada "to enter into agreements with the Provincial governments to pay them contributions toward their expenditures on social assistance and welfare," by way of F.P.F.T..

In the Supreme Court, the question which counsel and the court seemed to think needed to be decided was whether or not an amendment to the C.A.P., which had reduced the Federal government's contributions to provincial welfare programs was constitutional. The case was argued by counsel for the Attorneys-General of Canada, B.C., Ontario, Manitoba, Alberta and Saskatchewan, none of whom argued that the C.A.P. itself was beyond Parliament's authority and accordingly *ultra vires*. Counsel for Manitoba argued only that Parliament lacked legislative jurisdiction to make the proposed changes. How exactly Parliament could have had the jurisdiction to enact C.A.P. in the first place, but having done so, could not then change it, was not addressed, either by counsel or by the Court. It goes without saying that both counsel and the Court were entirely ignorant of the relevance of the Quebec Conference, and the relevant case law.

Sopinka's ended the judgment with this absolutely ludicrous statement:

> *"Finally, I turn to the second branch of this argument of the Attorney General of Manitoba. This was the argument that the*

---

[99] (1991) 2 S.C.R. 525.

"overriding principles of federalism" requires that Parliament be unable to interfere in areas of provincial jurisdiction. It was said that, in order to protect the autonomy of the provinces, the Court should supervise the Federal government's exercise of its spending power. But supervision of the spending power is not a separate head of judicial review. If a statute is neither ultra vires nor contrary to the Canadian Charter of Rights and Freedoms, the courts have no jurisdiction to supervise the exercise of legislative power."

The only explanation for Sopinka's nonsensical[100] statement, I can think of, is that he relied upon C.L.O.C.'s assertion that "spending," unlike "compulsory regulation," did not require authorizing legislation a statement which is not only demonstratively false but is contradicted by C.L.O.C. itself (in section 1.9) which cites the 1924 *Auckland Harbour Board* decision[101] of the Privy Council (quoted in the Introduction).

Here again, is the law as stated by the Privy Council, and endorsed by C.L.O.C.:

"It has been a principle of the British Constitution now for more than two centuries ... that no money can be taken out of the consolidated Fund into which the revenues of the state have been paid, excepting under a distinct authorization from Parliament itself."

The principle applied by the Privy Council in the *Auckland Harbour* case was a principle of the British Constitution which has existed for three centuries and has never been doubted. As "no money can be taken out of the (Federal government's) Consolidated fund ... excepting under a distinct authorization from parliament *itself*," it is clear beyond all possibility of doubt that with the rejection of Macdonald's motion in 1864 (which is reflected in the terms of the *BNA Act*) F.P.F.T. are not authorized by the Canadian constitution and F.P.F.T. are entirely illegitimate, as the *BNA Act* prohibits Parliament from authorizing them.

---

100 In the interests of full disclosure I should state that John Sopinka was a friend and classmate of mine at the University of Toronto School of Law and a very good lawyer. Nonetheless, this statement does not make any sense. The court is obliged to strike down *all ultra vires* government activities including the unlawful spending of taxpayers' money.

101 (1924) A.C. 318.

Yet in section 6.8(a) of C.L.O.C. all of this is forgotten and the C.A.P. decision of the Supreme Court is given as an authority for the clearly untenable conclusion that "there is no compelling reason to confine (federal) ... spending ... within the limits of (federal) legislative power because in those functions the government is not purporting to exercise any peculiarly governmental authority over its subjects."

If, as C.L.O.C. states correctly in its section 1.9 (in the passage quoted above) "*only Parliament (can) levy taxes ... an only Parliament (can) authorize the expenditure of public funds,*" then the *Constitution of Canada* is a compelling reason *to confine* federal taxation and federal spending "*within the limits of ... (the Federal government's) legislative power.*"

It is obvious that if money raised by federal taxes is raised to fund F.P.F.T. it is also obvious that those taxes must have been lawfully imposed by valid legislation. As the Privy Council stated in the *Insurance Act* case:[102]

> "The Parliament of Canada cannot by purporting to exercise taxation powers under s. 91, head 3, appropriate to itself exclusively a field of jurisdiction in which, apart from such a procedure it could exert no legal authority ... we know from Silver Brothers[103] that federal and provincial tax revenue are separated one from the other into two separate statutory purses."

The two separate statutory purses are clearly the federal purse which is governed by section 102 and designated as the repository for money to be appropriated for the Public Service of Canada and not for the public service of any province. The appreciation of this simple distinction is alone, sufficient to make it obvious that any and all federal taxes imposed in order to fund F.P.F.T. are funded from the wrong purse.

Nowhere in C.L.O.C.'s arguments made to justify F.P.F.T. is this point recognized, let alone dealt with C.L.O.C.'s section 31 is devoted to "Taxation." That section, states:

> "... the validity of the law imposing taxations turns on whether

---

102 In *re The Insurance Act of Canada* (1932) A.C. 41 at 53.
103 (1924) A.C. 318.

the enacting legislative body had legislative authority over the true matter of the law. The enacting body's taxing power is irrelevant."

That being the case, determining that federal taxation imposed to fund F.P.F.T. is *ultra vires* is as easy as "shooting ducks in a barrel." In the complete absence from C.L.O.C. of any mention of sections 102 and 126 of the *BNA Act*, and the omission of both from its Appendix advertised as the *Constriction Act 1867*, there is nothing more to be said.

CHAPTER 5
CONCLUSION

WHEN, in 1955, I began my time as a student at the University of Toronto's School of Law, my father was one of the nine Judges of the Supreme Court of Canada. I remember the advice he gave me then. He said that as a law student and hopefully a lawyer thereafter, I would be required to undertake a great deal of legal research. He said that whenever I did embark upon a task of research, I must "exhaust it," as that was the only way to be confident of the accuracy of the conclusions the research led to. Unfortunately, the author of C.L.O.C. did not do that.

As noted before, C.L.O.C.'s conclusion that the federal spending power "is nowhere explicit in the *Constitution Act 1867*" is balderdash. Sections 102 and 126 of the *Constitution Act 1867* explicitly limit both the spending power of Parliament and that of the provincial legislatures to the Public Service of Canada in the first case and those of the provincial legislatures, to the public service of the Provinces in the latter. The only exception to those limits is section 118 which was replaced by Section 1 of the *Constitution Act* 1907. That section provided for F.P.F.T. in amounts which are no longer significant. The only other relevant provision to be found in the Constitution is section 36 of the *Constitution Act 1982*, which I have already dealt with.

C.L.O.C.'s assertion that a federal spending power authorizing F.P.F.T.

must be inferred, is also balderdash in the light of the existence of section 102. It is impossible to interpret the Canadian Constitution according to the intent of "them that made it" without being aware of what the Fathers decided in 1864 at Quebec, which was confirmed at the London Conference held shortly before the bill which became the *BNA Act* was introduced in the Parliament at Westminster. Yet nowhere in C.L.O.C. can you find any reference to either the Quebec or London Conferences. In particular, in reference to Macdonald's motion of October 21, 1864 cannot be found anywhere in C.L.O.C..

———

As we have seen, on October 21, 1864 at the Quebec Conference, John A. Macdonald moved that what became section 91 of the *BNA Act*, should include in the list of powers to be conferred on the Parliament of Canada the authority "to make laws", "respecting … subsidies or grants in aid of the …" Provincial governments and the Fathers of Confederation deliberately refused to do so. How the author of C.L.O.C. could suggest in the light of that indisputable fact that such a power must now be inferred is a mystery. The Constitution does not contain any such provisions and no judge, law professor or anyone else has the ability to change history.

It is evident that the author of C.L.O.C is ignorant of that history, but ignorance cannot be a basis for re-writing the Constitution so as to satisfy the ideological preferences of anyone including law professors.

Whether they or anyone else would like to see a Constitution which would make F.P.F.T. lawful is utterly and completely irrelevant. To contend (as C.L.O.C. does) that the Parliament of Canada has a limitless power to transfer federal tax-payers money to the governments of the Provinces is a hoax.

www.ingramcontent.com/pod-product-compliance
Lightning Source LLC
Chambersburg PA
CBHW071909070526
44583CB00016B/1907